Dedicated
to my mother

"Flowers, plants and fishes,
   beasts, birds, flies and bees,
Hills, dales, plains, pastures,
   skies, seas, rivers, trees.
There's nothing near at hand
   or fartherest sought
But with the needle may
   be shaped and wrought."

The Needle's Excellency
by John Taylor (1580-1653)

The Art of

CREWEL EMBROIDERY

by MILDRED J. DAVIS

CROWN PUBLISHERS, INC., NEW YORK

INSTRUCTION MANUALS BY MILDRED J. DAVIS

Simplified Approach to Rug Hooking

Crewel Techniques for Rug Patterns

Library of Congress Catalog Card Number: 62-11810
ISBN: 0-517-016060
ISBN: 0-517-500779 pbk
Printed in the United States of America

Jacket illustration designed and embroidered by the author.

Thirteenth Printing, March, 1976

Title page illustration: a section from a petticoat border made in New England, 1725-1750.
Courtesy Boston Museum of Fine Arts.

ACKNOWLEDGMENTS

This book could not have been written without considerable expenditure of time and effort on the part of my husband. Before the actual writing stage there were two friends—Irving and Natalie Kaden—whose persistent badgerings induced me to translate class notes into chapters. And, even earlier, there was Mrs. Clifford S. Jones, who first introduced me to the fascinations of crewel embroidery.

My appreciation also goes to Mildred C. Howes, to Wendell Smith, to Barbara C. Waddell and my sisters, Frances J. Mason and Helen J. Kramer, for their sustaining interest and encouragement, and to my two children, Patricia and Wingfield, Jr., who have stoically endured the disruptions of a household wracked by a book-in-progress.

There are special niches for Louise Hinchliffe and local photographers and artists, including Bela Kalman and Joanne Bliss, who helped to provide necessary illustrations, charts, diagrams and drawings, to Margery Kronengold, who designed this book and contributed many of the ornamental drawings, and to Helen E. Sterling of Crown Publishers, Inc., a skilled coordinator.

Many friends who own fine pieces of crewel embroidery, some of which is their own personal handiwork, have been generous in lending photographs of their property for use in the book. To the museums and institutions—including the Museum of Fine Arts in Boston, the Royal Ontario Museum in Toronto, the Victoria and Albert Museum in London; the Metropolitan Museum of Art and the Museum for the Arts of Decoration of Cooper Union in New York, the Heritage Foundation in Deerfield, Mass., the Essex Institute in Salem, Mass.: the Wadsworth Atheneum in Hartford, Conn.; the Tryon Palace Restoration in New Bern, N. C., the Henry Francis Du Pont Winterthur Museum in Winterthur, Del., and Colonial Williamsburg in Virginia; to publications and publishers—including *House Beautiful, Interiors, McCall's Needlework & Crafts,* Sir Isaac Pitman & Sons, Ltd. and Studio Books, Ltd.; to firms, organizations and individuals—including Arthur H. Lee, Ltd., Appleton Bros., Ltd.; William Briggs and Company, Ltd.; Mrs. Joan Toggitt; D. M. C Corporation; Paternayan Brothers and the New York Arthritis and Rheumatism Foundation—my sincere appreciation also for allowing me to reproduce examples of crewelwork and other items from their collections.

CONTENTS

ILLUSTRATIONS

Color Plates 🌿 *(following page 64)*

Halftones 🌿

PROLOGUE

Author's Note: If you like, why not browse a bit first? Then, when you are ready to embark upon your own adventures in crewel embroidery, come back to the Prologue and start from here.

Decorative needlework is acknowledged as one of the most universal forms of self-expression, spanning many centuries of human history and embracing a wide variety of societies and cultures, from gaudy savage finery to the intricate traceries of an eighteenth-century waistcoat. Crewel embroidery stands high as one of the most diverse, colorful, exciting and demanding of the traditional needle arts.

The charm and repose of crewel work through many generations can best be demonstrated in a pictorial gallery of outstanding examples, and many antique and modern pieces have been selected as illustrations for this book. Yet any woman today, inspired by the craftsmanship of the past, can undertake a crewel design to enhance her own home. Although advice and assistance in such a personal undertaking is the main subject of this book, the fascinating story of crewel embroidery should not be passed over entirely. It came to a rich flowering during an age of unprecedented expansion in western civilization. Almost every traditional crewel motif originally reflected some current vogue or tide of events. A survey of the well-deserved popularity of crewel embroidery both in the Old World and the New should add its own subtle dimension to your enjoyment of this graceful art.

Following the brief history you will find information about the basic materials you will need for crewel embroidery, as well as simple techniques for transferring designs onto the background cloth. Then you will find a concise discussion of the principles of color harmony—just detailed enough to help you embroider your first piece of crewel embroidery in monochrome (shades of a single color). This piece will involve only the simplest of stitches, some of which you may already know or can easily learn in half an hour. After finishing it you will see for yourself that crewel embroidery need not be elaborate in order to be attractive, although many of the subsequent designs will employ much more detail than this introductory example.

After you become more at ease with needle and hoop, you will be ready for a design that employs more than one color. You will learn more about color harmony and color balancing by selecting certain value sequences of colored yarn from a color chart. After this adventure in polychrome (a combination of several colors) your advance into larger, more colorful designs requiring an increased repertoire of embroidery stitches, will be rapid. Your rate of progress is up to you.

Along the way you will find suggestions about the choice of yarns, their arrangement for ease in handling, the enlargement or reduction of pattern sizes to fit special needs, the adaptation of crewel designs to articles suitable for home or personal use and the methods used to ensure proper finishing and blocking of completed embroideries—just about every phase you are likely to encounter in creating contemporary versions of this exquisite art. Not every crewel piece, of course, may prove compatible with a modern decorating scheme, but in many cases the special appeal of crewel embroidery may provide an appropriate color accent for your room.

The two major reference sections in this book—the group of stitches, shown in photographs and diagrams, and the collection of design units—are in fact treasuries of traditional elements, with full descriptions provided of step-by-step techniques for reproducing the charming old mounds, trees, leaves, fruits, flowers and animals that contribute to the charm of crewel embroidery. You will probably want to return to these storehouses again and again for inspiration as your technical skills improve and your imagination seeks fuller scope.

Following the treasury of design units is still another storehouse, to be savored and browsed through at your pleasure. It identifies the rich plant and animal life, both real and imaginary, most often encountered in crewel embroidery, with brief commentaries embodying piquant emblematic and symbolic associations. Much of this material comes from the pen of contemporary observers, whose comments in a quaint and frequently pungent vein provide thoroughly delightful diversions.

Working in crewel wools has richly rewarded the efforts of those persevering needlewomen who have mastered the fundamentals sufficiently to be able to integrate its charm into a setting of their choice. Basic personal motivations—the desire for self-expression and the desire to surround one's family with beauty—are sustained and nurtured in this endlessly fascinating form of fine needlework. Crewel embroidery offers one of the most diverse, most interesting and most available avenues to creative accomplishment.

This book has not been evolved to lead you into a wilderness of color theory, esoteric stitches or extravagant design. One common denominator—simplicity—is threaded through all observations on the use (and abuse) of color, the repertoire of stitches and the storehouse of design units and composite designs. With a good understanding of basic principles you can go as far as you like in experimenting with color, design and stitch combinations. A flexible, highly creative medium is yours for the taking. Do try it—and enjoy it.

There is but one thing more to say: Even as the preparation of this book has added a broad new dimension to my pleasure in creative embroidery, I wish it may enhance your own enjoyment of this rewarding art.

Mildred J. Davis
Chestnut Hill, Mass.

CHAPTER ONE

THE TIDES OF HISTORY
AND THE COURSE OF CREWEL

To attempt a definitive history of crewel embroidery—or any other embroidery, for that matter—is to undertake an almost impossible task.

The coronations of monarchs, the signing of treaties, the usurpations of dictators, the depositions of tyrants have all been noted by contemporary chroniclers. Not so with embroideries. There were no treaties, no tyrants but fashion, and although every skilled embroiderer was queen in her own realm she more often than not neglected to identify and date her work.

Thus one is left with a few scattered facts, some circumstantial evidence, much conjecture, and enough conflicting interpretations by recognized authorities to give pause to any who may be tempted to make dogmatic pronouncements. From this material the following notes on the history of crewel embroidery have been compiled in order to capture for you some of the background color of the eras which gave this lovely art its distinctive quality. These notes contain various items of his-

torical information, some of them seemingly without immediate relevance to the subject of crewel embroidery. On reflection, however, one may begin to recognize an underlying pertinence.

Embroidery is truly an art of the people. To understand it, an embroiderer should know something of the people who created it, of the events which affected their daily life and of the circumstances and prevailing styles of decoration which influenced their designs, their materials and techniques.

The use of wool threads in embroidery goes back at least a thousand years. Perhaps the most famous example of wool embroidery is the Bayeux Tapestry which, despite its name, is actually embroidery, and which is still displayed in Bayeux today. The exact date of this work is not known, but most authorities fix it within a few years after the Battle of Hastings. This remarkable canvas, approximately 230 feet long by 20 inches wide, depicts the Norman conquest of England, climaxed by the Battle of Hastings in October 1066. Its uncomplicated story-telling technique has an instantaneous appeal for any viewer—familiar scenes mingled with the fast pace and drama of battle, touches of ribald humor and, for those few who could read, explanatory legends in Latin.

The identity of the embroiderer, or embroiderers, is likewise shrouded in mystery, but some antiquaries believe it to have been the work of Mathilda, wife of William the Conqueror; others incline to the view that it was executed under the direction of Matilda, daughter of Henry I. The technique is unusual: colored wools have been worked on a background of bleached linen. Stitches include laid work, couching, stem and outline. The work itself is characterized by close attention to exact detail.

The oldest manuscript-reference to this embroidery was found in the 1476 inventory of treasures owned by the Church of Notre Dame in Bayeux. No further mention of it is known until 1724 when, apparently for the first time, it attracted attention outside the parish. Presumably, it reposed in the archives of the church during all those years.

Worsted yarns have long been used in many European countries to create lovely embroideries, some of which have been preserved in museum collections. Several fine examples of Continental origin are included in this book. Crewel embroidery, however, had its roots and owes its name, its motifs, its traditions and its techniques to the life of sixteenth- and seventeenth-century England. It is this particular background that will be discussed in some detail here.

The initial period of development, lasting about 100 years and ending near the mid-seventeenth century, was succeeded by a period of full flowering which edged into the eighteenth century. Crewel embroidery was heir to all embroidery tradition that had gone before, with such predecessors as panels and robes designed for church use and fine garments and hangings.

One of the earliest references to crewel work by that name is found in a sixteenth-century household inventory: "a lytle stoole covered withe Nedle worcke checkerid withe white, blewe & tawnye cruell." Unfortunately, the "lytle stoole" and the inventory list have been separated along the avenues of time, so one cannot positively identify the type of embroidery. The word "checkerid" suggests the tent stitch, or what is today called needlepoint.

Is it surprising that crewel embroidery is associated with the art of needlepoint? The word "crewel" (or "crule," or "cruell," as it has been variously spelled) was not originally used to identify a form of embroidery; it simply meant a worsted yarn of two threads used primarily for tapestry and embroidery. Any form of embroidery done in worsted yarns could be spoken of as crewel work. Modern dictionaries still define crewel as a type of yarn used for embroidery, but more and more the term "crewel embroidery" evokes an image of the specific type of embroidery described and illustrated in this book.

The use of the word "crewel" in everyday speech in seventeenth-century England is vouched for by a number of contemporary writers. In Sir Izaak Walton's *The Compleat Angler* (1653) one finds "A May-flie, you may make his body of greenish-coloured crewels." In *King Lear* (1606) Shakespeare had his Fool exclaim, "Ha ha! He wears cruel garters." This was a pun on crewel garters, which were then often worn, as noted by Ben Jonson in *The Alchemist* (1610): "Ere we contribute a new crewel garter To his most worsted worship." Also in a punning vein, from *Woman's A Weathercock* (1612) comes this: "Wearing of silk, why art thou so cruel?" The word was well known, and obviously did not refer to embroidery.

English embroideries, especially ecclesiastical works, were renowned throughout the civilized world during the Middle Ages. About 1400 the quality of this work began to decline and remained in a rather forlorn state for about 150 years until near the beginning of the Elizabethan Age. Then it sprang forth again, more vigorously alive than ever.

One bright spot during the twilight years was the introduction of the invaluable steel needle to England. Steel-needle manufacturing, said to be a Chinese contribution, was centered in Nuremberg about 1370 and from there gradually spread throughout Europe. Just when the steel needle found its way to England is not known, but they were first manufactured there about 1545.

The renaissance of English embroidery came during a period marked by widely different religious and political passions within the realm and bold ventures in the New World across the sea. Its development was linked with events both at home and abroad, with changes in daily life brought in their wake and with the influence on the fashions of the day exerted by the procession of successive rulers. Beginning with the reign of Elizabeth I and continuing through that of Queen Anne a century and a half later, some of the major forces which left an imprint on the art of crewel embroidery are briefly outlined.

Elizabeth I (1558-1603)* was a Tudor, daughter of Henry VIII and Anne Boleyn. When Elizabeth was three her mother was beheaded and her father, to clear the way for another marriage, pressed Parliament to declare his marriage to Anne Boleyn invalid *ab initio* (from the beginning), an act which placed the stamp of illegitimacy upon Elizabeth. In his will, however, Henry VIII named Elizabeth as his rightful heir in line of succession after his other two children, Mary and Edward. The line of succession included also Mary Stuart, known as Mary Queen of Scots, immediately following Elizabeth, should she die without a legitimate heir.

The union of Scotland and England was ardently desired by some and as violently opposed by others. Much blood had already been shed in abortive forays by both sides. In addition to political rivalries religious conflicts mounted. Scandalmongers soon made much of Mary Queen of Scots'

* Note: The years in brackets indicate the years of various sovereigns' reigns.

indiscretions and her alleged implication in the murder of her second husband Lord Darnley. Partisans on both sides continued to hurl charges of bastardy and murderous adultery in the vigorous language of the day. With such turmoil in the land, it is quite likely that when embroiderers expressed personal sympathies by working Tudor roses or Stuart carnations into their embroideries they did so with passionate convictions.

But all was not blood, violence and intrigue. The people of this lusty age were expanding their horizons in many new directions, busy building homes, schools and churches, exploring the world beyond their shores, expanding their overseas trade, busy making money and gaily, madly acquiring material possessions and amusing themselves on holidays. They were also strengthening their power by rough-hewing and polishing their legislative jewel, parliamentary government.

They were God-fearing, yet receptive to all manner of superstitions. They were sometimes intolerant in their religious beliefs, yet amid the bigotry there lay the seeds of a great milestone in the struggle against the abuse of arbitrary authority, the habeas corpus act. They were splendidly insulated—until 1588—against fear of invasion and conquest; they were deeply nationalistic, fanatic in defense of their freedoms, ruggedly individualistic, noisy, ostentatious, lacking in subtlety, frequently uncouth, contemptuous of foreigners yet generous in offering sanctuary to refugees fleeing the bitter strife of the Continent. Foreigners did not always share the Englishman's exalted opinion of himself. A traveler from the Continent acknowledged them to be "good sailors . . . and even better pirates," as well as "cunning, treacherous and knavish." The English found such a description most unjust but apropos as applied to any other people.

The Elizabethans relished sport, and a startling degree of physical violence was present in many of their outdoor games. Broken heads, limbs, ribs and necks were accepted as ordinary hazards of an afternoon of vigorous fun. They vastly enjoyed cards, dicing and gaming and were not always completely scrupulous. They loved gay clothes, fancy gloves and jewelry, fairs, dancing, cockfights, fireworks, masques, the theater. In quieter moments they sang, were often quite accomplished in the playing of musical instruments and read avidly everything that came to hand. They had an insatiable curiosity about anything anywhere.

Shakespeare described them in his *Richard II:*

This happy breed of men, this little world,
This precious stone set in the silver sea,
This blessed plot, this earth, this realm,
             this England,

Widening prosperity was creating a tremendous new social force—an expanding, articulate middle class. A much broader segment of society was finding the leisure, the money, the incentives to turn its growing talents to a form of creative effort: that of decorating homes and apparel. No longer were embroidering skills immured within religious institutions, the royal palaces or the homes of the wealthy. A vital force was building which was destined to have a deep and significant influence upon the needle arts.

How, then, did the Elizabethan embroiderer make use of her talents, what were her materials and from where did her inspirations spring? Her home was likely to be drafty, her furniture massive, cumbersome and barren of upholstery. Undoubtedly, her primary concern was to make the house a more comfortable place. To accomplish this she needed warm, practical items such as floor carpets, table "carpets," covers for chairs, benches, window seats, hangings, curtains, bed testers, valances, spreads and cushions, followed perhaps by pieces with less emphasis on utility such as "sweet bagges" (sachets), book covers, pincushions, embroidered pictures, etc. Touches of colorful embroidery were much admired by her family on bodices, jackets, hoods, coifs, stomachers, nightcaps, gloves, purses and bags.

Much of this "fine sewing" was done by the lady of the house, assisted by such skilled help as she could obtain, including her daughters or relatives within the household. The more affluent could afford and often employed the services of professional embroiderers—usually men—who were acknowledged as skilled craftsmen and in time formed a guild of their own, called the Broderers' Company.

Most of the household pieces were worked in silk, or silk and wool and almost invariably on canvas or linen canvas. Very little embroidery was done wholly in wool, and very little of the ground material had a twill weave. Costume embroidery was most often done on linen, velvet, satin or silk. Designs were worked almost entirely in silk or combinations of silk and silver or silver-gilt threads. There was no crewel embroidery in the modern sense.

Linen and canvas materials were partly domestic and partly imported, with the best-quality materials coming from the Continent. Silks were brought in by Levantine traders and were probably available to the housewife already dyed in various colors. Wool yarns were domestic in origin, often spun in the home.

The Elizabethan embroiderer used an impressive variety of stitches in her craft: back, basket, braid, plaited braid, brick, buttonhole, chain, coral, cross, long-armed cross, French knot, herringbone, link, long and short, running, double running, satin, seed, split, stem, tent as well as laid work and couching.

Nor was her choice of colors scant. In addition to black, white, yellow, purple, silver and gold she had ashe, greene, peache, marigolde, orenge, pinke, redde, crymson, blewe, straw-colour and others intriguingly described as horse-fleshe, ladie-blushe, Isabella-colour, brasell, wachet, heare-colour, murrey, tawnye. These last six are light buff, a variety of red, light blue, hair color, purple-red or mulberry and orange-brown respectively. This does not exhaust the list. Elizabethans liked their colors bright, rich and vigorous.

Inspiration came from several sources: from pieces wrought by prior generations, from emblem books, illustrated Bibles and the few pattern-books then available, but, most importantly, from the land itself—its trees, fruits, flowers, insects, birds, animals. Some descriptive books were devoted to animals, birds and insects, with natural or fanciful illustrations. These sources, although not designed for use in embroidery, were undoubtedly used in traditional crewel embroidery designs. The great source of inspiration was the world at their feet. Sixteenth-century Europeans had a tremendous interest in the world and everything about it, an interest and enthusiasm reflected by Elizabethan embroiderers in their floral and arboreal designs. They delighted in their green land and all its bounty, in their gardens, their forests, their fields and all creatures great and small dwelling therein. Gerard,° a contemporary herbalist, asked proudly, "What greater delight is there than to behold the earth apparelled with plants, as with a robe of embroidered work?"

Of fruits and flowers their designs had a wealth of carnations, columbine, cornflowers, daffodils, honeysuckle, lilies, marigolds, pansies, pinks, primroses, snowdrops, thistles, tulips, violets, pea-pods, acorns, currants, grapes, domestic nuts, pomegranates and strawberries. Not all the flowers in the early designs are precisely identifiable, some perhaps because of inadequacy of technique and others because they may have been just simple random flowers without real counterparts in nature.

From the animal and insect kingdoms they drew upon hares, lions, foxes, frogs, stags, rabbits, snails, owls, falcons, parrots, pelicans, various domestic birds, eagles, beetles, moths, dragonflies, caterpillars and flies. Many of these, especially the flowers and fruits, were native to England's heath. The pomegranate, of course, is a notable exception, as are the lion and parrot. These exceptions probably came from the descriptions of flora in Gerard's *Herbal* or one of the animal books or bestiaries.

° John Gerard, English surgeon and botanist (1545-1612), author of *The Herbal: Generall Historie of Plantes,* London, 1597. For a time Gerard was superintendent of Lord Burghley's gardens; later he had his own gardens near Shakespeare's home.

The tides of history flowed swiftly on. In the 1560's the Puritans first became evident as a force to be reckoned with. In 1564 a towering figure of the English Renaissance—William Shakespeare—was born in Stratford-on-Avon. In 1568 Mary Queen of Scots was unseated and fled to England, there to live 18 years in "protective custody." She was charged with complicity in a plot against Elizabeth I, tried, condemned and eventually beheaded. Thus, her son, James VI of Scotland, took his place next after Elizabeth in the line of succession to the English throne.

In 1570 Elizabeth was excommunicated, an act which, in a sense, cut England adrift from the Continent even if it did not place her beyond reach of the two great powers, France and Spain. Fortunately for England, France and Spain were too busy with intrigues against each other to unite in a common cause. Elizabeth exercised all her considerable talents playing one against the other and thus won time to rebuild her first line of defense, the Royal Navy, and to reinforce commercial ramparts at home and abroad. With shrewdness and foresight she guided her country through peril, relying on her own judgment and that of her valued counselors, as probably no man of that era could have done.

In 1582 part of the world took a ten-day step forward when it adopted the Gregorian calendar, which made up for a full ten-day lapse behind sun time by having October 15th thenceforth follow October 4th. The English, however, waited 170 years to adopt the new dating system. In 1585 Sir Francis Drake girdled the globe. His feat was a warning to the Spanish that they would soon have a rival for supremacy of the high seas. The showdown was not to be postponed for long. In that same era Sir Walter Raleigh sent forth a party to establish the first English settlement in the New World. That lost colony disappeared from the face of the earth, save for three names—Croatan, Roanoke, Virginia Dare.

The Elizabethan Age saw the introduction of two plants of the New World to the daily life of the Old: the potato and tobacco. Both were to become staple items of consumption. The potato flower was to be enshrined in embroidery motifs, but the tobacco flower was never so recognized unless, perchance, it may be masquerading somewhere under the pseudonym "padula" (imaginative flower).

In 1588 the great Spanish Armada—131 large ships, together with a covey of smaller ones and more than 20,000 men poised for invasion—was hurled back. English seapower was now in the ascendancy, abetted no little by nautical entrepreneurs and able seamen who discerned the twin virtues of patriotism and profit in piratical excursions, virtues thrice savored if the victims chanced to be Spanish.

In 1600 the East India Company was chartered, and with it a decisive penetration of the Orient began. A controversy has grown up around the role of the East India Company and the sources for the exotic designs to be found in some examples of crewel embroidery. This will be taken up shortly.

In 1603 Queen Elizabeth's long reign came to an end and James, son of Mary Stuart, came to the throne as James I of England. At last England and Scotland were united under one head. As the sixteenth century drew to a close many of the distinctive elements that were to appear in crewel work had been introduced. In design the detached floral motifs, coiling stems and branches had all been well defined. The "exotic" flowers, lavishly worked, oversized leaves, the popular Tree of Life motif, the mounds, the subtle oriental influences were yet to be fully developed, but pattern trends destined to be closely identified with crewel embroidery in succeeding years were clearly discernible. Of course, it must be remembered that there were no historians at hand to jot down notes about such trends. Therefore, in attempting any summation of the development of crewel embroidery at this stage, it should be stated that while some of the conclusions to follow seem self-evident, others are born of fragmentary observations and are presented in the guise of honest conjecture.

It was during the first quarter of the seventeenth century that suggestions of oriental exoticism in domestic embroideries developed to a noticeable degree. Tudor taste had run to profusion; few embroiderers could resist filling all available areas with ornament. Yet in some instances the Elizabethan embroiderer seemed to recognize that graceful open spaces had their own peculiar charms. Most of the flora and fauna characteristic of crewel embroidery had already been introduced to the embroiderer's needle. Those yet to be brought into the fold included the harebell, Canterbury bell, foxglove, wheat, peacock, bird of paradise, snake, dog, leopard and the butterfly. Only a few stitches not general to the Elizabethan repertoire later appeared with some frequency in crewel embroideries: bullion, double coral, feather and thorn.

Embroidered pieces, large and small, were prized possessions, not created nor disposed of casually. Creating them required hard-learned skills, much time and patience and materials not easily come by. Months, even years, of labor often went into some of the larger, more elaborate works. Consequently the bequeathing of such properties as embroideries was seldom left to chance. Great care was taken to place them where they would be appreciated and well cared for. Embroideries were treasures in a real sense of the word and were accorded the respect reserved for precious belongings.

Carnation (clove gillyflower). Early seventeenth century, silk embroidery on linen. Long and short, stem, herringbone and satin stitches, laid work and couching. *Courtesy Victoria & Albert Museum*, Flowers in English Embroidery.

The will drawn up by Dame Anne Sherley of London, shows the care with which embroideries were inventoried in a last will and testament.

> "...a long cushion and chaire of needlework of apples.
> ...sixe of my high stooles of silke needlework.
> ...my chaire of silke needlework.
> ...five of my chairs of cruell needlework.
> ...my carpet of needlework of gillyflores and woodbyns.
> ...my Turkey carpet of cowcumbers.
> ...my square carpet of Turkey worke wroughte into piramids and trafles.
> ...a long cushion of trafles with severall beasts thereon ymbroydered.
> ...my carpett of hawthornes and other flowers with a black ground.
> ...a square bord carpet of woodbyns.
> ...My Turkey-worke carpett on the longest table in the dyning roome at London.
> ...a cupbord carpet of thistles."

For those who are not familiar with old plant names, it may be helpful to note that gillyflores (or gillyflowers) was a name applied to many flowers with a scent suggesting that of cloves. Woodbyns (woodbine) was an early name for various climbing plants such as ivy, or sometimes honeysuckle. Trafles (or trefoils) might refer to a plant with three leaves such as clover or a yellow-flowered plant of the trefoil family.

James I, who reigned from 1603 to 1625, was identified in the formal Latin style of the day as "Jacobus Britanniae Rex." From this, of course, it is but a step to the phrase "Jacobean," but immediately a curious paradox asserts itself. Why should this phrase be associated with a distinctive type of embroidery that did not attain widespread popularity until some four decades after James I's death?

The phrase "Jacobean" is defined, in the *Oxford English Dictionary*, as "of or pertaining to the reign or time of James I, especially architecture, also a statesman or writer at the time of James I." The people gave an informal emphasis to the word by calling the first gold coins (1603) to bear the new king's name (Jacobus Rex) "jacobuses," although officially they were sovereigns. The *Oxford Dictionary* dates the first use of "Jacobean" as applied to the James I era as 1844. In any case, "Jacobean" connotes the period marking the development of exotic design in English embroidery. Yet the term is not wholly appropriate in this country since its connotations are entirely English, and since American influences on the development of crewel embroidery are also considered here, "crewel embroidery" has been used in preference to "Jacobean embroidery."

The origin of oriental influences in English embroidery design is in itself a fascinating study. For many years India was commonly thought to be the source. This was presumed to be the result of the importation by the East India Company of vast quantities of painted cottons called palimpores from India. These cottons were polychrome and featured many of the motifs later associated closely with crewel embroidery: variations on the Tree of Life theme, with hillocks and occasional small animals in the foreground, large veined leaves with curled or notched edges and exotic flowers. According to the long-held theory the new imports were instantly popular in England and these strange and fascinating designs began to be incorporated in domestic embroideries.

It is interesting to note that in support of this older theory the Oriental or "chinoiserie" elements of these printed cottons are often singled out, particularly the birds and animals. "Chinoiserie" was not truly Oriental but actually a European-English concept of Chinese motifs interpreted without benefit of disciplined skills in the idiom; in short, a western paraphrase of the authentic Chinese style. But all those interested in the real direction of the current, whether from east or west, are indebted to Mr. John Irwin, historian of Indian art at the Victoria and Albert Museum, London, for a new insight into the origin of oriental influences in English embroideries. His studies of early East India Company records led to conclusions quite contrary to the previously accepted explanation. His research led to the following interpretation of events.

The turbaned hunters equipped with bows and arrows suggest Oriental influences in this crewelwork panel embroidered on twill-woven linen and cotton. English, seventeenth century. *Courtesy Colonial Williamsburg, Williamsburg, Va.*

First, the earliest records of the East India Company refer not to textile imports from India but to English *embroideries* sent out to India. This was in response to a demand for Jacobean embroideries, which were much in favor there until about 1617. Thus, it would appear, Irwin states, that the first exchange of design ideas flowed from England to India, not the other way around. This is given additional weight by Company records showing that importation of Indian textiles did not attain massive proportions until after 1660. In addition to sending complete embroideries to India, designs including such pastoral motifs as shepherds with staffs were sent out to India to be embroidered there and returned to England. Many Indians were highly skilled craftsmen, but somehow the shepherds sprouted turbans and flowing robes. It is amusing to speculate whether the English recognized their own patterns when they came back home. Of course when Indian craftsmen "translated" English patterns into their own textiles they probably gave the finished products enough oriental flavor to suggest a slightly exotic appearance to English eyes.

A second point raised by Mr. Irwin is the unlikelihood that Chinese influences would appear in designs originating in India. The two cultures did not overlap to any great extent, therefore "chinoiserie" elements in Indian textiles could not have resulted from adoption of Chinese motifs into native Indian patterns. It would appear more likely, then, he continues, that the Indian craftsmen were merely executing patterns suggested to them or adopted by them for practical commercial reasons. What more natural than that Indians should make use of English designs in textiles made for export to England? East India Company records would seem to confirm this point.

This leaves unanswered the question of how oriental influences originally became available to England for export to India. There appears to be no simple, clear-cut, well-documented answer, but there are clues here and there. For about 300 years silks from China had been a highly valued item carried by the caravans following the ancient trade routes through India and Persia and thence into Europe. In the early 1500's the Portuguese opened sea lanes to the Far East and greatly increased Europe's exposure to China and the Orient. Other maritime powers soon joined the quest. By 1600 Europeans—and the English—were well acquainted with goods from the Far East, especially spices and silks. Apparently they found the oriental idiom thoroughly delightful and, in attempting to translate it to their own decorative uses, developed "chinoiserie." Whatever its origin, the East has added its own peculiar charms to the heritage of embroidery tradition.

No clangor of war disturbed the peaceful reign of James I, but there were internal problems aplenty. He weathered them all but solved none—to the ultimate distress of the subsequent monarch. In the second year of the reign of James I the first English-language dictionary was published, bringing some degree of order to Elizabethan spellings, awesome samplings of private enterprise rampant. In 1611, after seven years of effort by a committee of eminent scholars, the King James Authorized Version of the Bible was completed. Perhaps no similar religious document has ever had so great an impact upon the course of a living language as this classic.

In 1607 came Jamestown; in 1620, Plymouth. At last the far-venturing English were gaining a permanent foothold upon the North American continent. It seems quite likely that some of these new settlers brought aboard ship some of their favorite bed-hangings or table "carpetts" as well as materials for others, to be completed during the long sea voyage that lay ahead. They did bring needles, thread, pieces of material and other such housewifery-essentials to keep their clothes and linens in repair. Could any woman, packing a sewing kit, close her heart to all the lovely reminders of a home she might never see again? At least the early colonists brought an affection for the bright embroideries that had graced their former rooms and the techniques for making their own.

Along with the English, Dutch traders and settlers were also drawn to the New World. They erected a fort and storehouse at what is now New York City in 1615 and negotiated the purchase of Manhattan Island from the Indians for 60 guilders. They were able to maintain peaceful relations with them for 25 years and prospered in their new colony with its fine harbor.

In 1621 Robert Burton provided, in his *Anatomie of Melancholy,* proof that women's fingers were seldom idle. "Now for women, instead of laborious studies they have curious needleworks, cutworks, spinning, bone-lace and many pretty devices of their own making, to adorn their houses, cushions, carpets, chairs, stools ('for she eats not the bread of idleness,' Proverbs xxxi. 27), confections, conserves, distillations, &c., which they show to strangers.

> "Which to her guests she shows, with all her pelf,
> Thus far my maids, but this I did myself."

"This they have to busy themselves about, household offices, &c., neat gardens, full of exotic, versicolour, diversely varied, sweet-smelling flowers and plants in all kinds, which they are most ambitious to get, curious to preserve and keep, proud to possess, and many much times brag of."

For their instruction Richard Shorleyker published in 1624 *A Schole-house for the Needle,* which he described in this manner: "Here followeth certaine Patterns of Cut-workes; newly invented and never published before. Also sundry spots as, Flowers, Birds, Fishes &c., and will fitly serve to be wrought, some in Gould, some in Silke, and some with Crewell in coullors; or otherwise at your pleasyure." It proved a popular work, with a second edition printed in 1632.

In 1625 James I died and his son came to the throne as Charles I (1625-1649). His was to be a troubled reign indeed. Almost immediately he became involved in wars with Spain and France. Violent disagreements with Parliament over fiscal problems, foreign policy, taxation and the rights of individual citizens led to dissolution of that body and 11 years of personal rule without their advice and consent.

The gentler passions of creative embroidery passed almost unscathed through these turmoils and found a contemporary chronicler in John Taylor,* customs officer on the Thames, pamphleteer and minor versifier. Called the "Water Poet," he was the author of *The Needle's Excellency.* This was described as "A New Booke wherein are divers admirable workes wrought with the needle. Newly invented and cut in copper for the pleasure and profit of the industrious." This popular volume ran through 12 editions, the first of uncertain date, the tenth published in 1634 and the twelfth in 1640.

Of his book Taylor went on to say:

* John Taylor, (1580-1653), author of *The Needle's Excellency* and various "travelogues" including *The Pennyles Pilgrimage,* or *The Moneylesse Perambulation of John Taylor, and How He Travailed from London to Edenborough in Scotland.*

Many of the early paper patterns literally fell apart after their outlines were traced and retraced or pricked and "pounced" (powdered charcoal was often sifted through the holes along the outlines onto the cloth upon which a

"This book some cunning workes doth teach,
(Too hard for meane capacities to reach)
So for weake learners, other workes here be,
As plaine and easie as are ABC."

The modern embroiderer is also indebted to Poet Taylor for his compilation of patterns, which were:

"Collected with much paine and industry,
From scorching Spaine and freezing Muscovy,
From fertill France and pleasant Italy,
From Polande, Sweden, Denmarke, Germany,
And some of these rare patternes have been set
Beyond the bounds of faithlesse Mahomet,
From spacious China and those Kingdomes East
And from great Mexico, and Indies West.
Thus are these workes farre fetch'd and dearly
   bought,
And consequently good for laydes thought."

India is not mentioned by name but might have been included by Taylor under "Kingdomes East." He also listed Workes that were fashionable and the many varied stitches which could be employed:

"For Tent-worke, Raisd-worke, Laid-worke, Frost-
   worke, New worke,
Most curious Purles, or rare Italian Cut-worke,
Fine Ferne-stitch, Finny-stitch, New-stitch and
   Chain-stitch,
Brave Bred-stitch, Fisher-stitch, Irish-stitch and
   Queene-stitch,

The Spanish-stitch, Rosemary-stitch and Mowse-
   stitch,
The smarting Whip-stitch, Back-stitch & the
   Crosse-stitch,
All these are good and these we must allow
And these are everywhere in practice now."

Some of these stitches are instantly recognizable; probably all of them could be identified on sight but, dressed in their quaint seventeenth-century names, some of them are "too hard for meane capacities to reach."

Not all the financial crises of the times could be laid at King Charles' door. Man's yen for a "fast jacobus" was well developed even then, as was amply demonstrated by the feverish speculation in tulips of the mid-1630's. At the peak of this mania prices rose as high as the equivalent of several thousands of dollars for a single tulip bulb. For those without such princely means of their own to invest, share plans were devised, a kind of early syndicate. As usual the unscrupulous were quick to capitalize upon the naïveté of the unwary by selling shares in non-existent bulbs. It was nothing less than incredible. When the bubble finally burst in 1637 many European households were in distress and bankruptcies attained record proportions.

It is not known whether speculations in tulips led to symbolic associations, but perhaps more than one gentlewoman at her embroidery frame may have contemplated the petals of this lovely flower with fond gratitude or with bitter regret, depending on the extent to which the family fortune had increased or diminished in the recent madness.

design was to be embroidered). These are a few of the "Patternes of Cut-workes" offered by Richard Shorleyker in his volume, *A Schole-house for the Needle.*

As the fourth decade of this century began, the tides of history seemed to sweep the English people into a maelstrom. The Tudor monarchs Henry VIII and Elizabeth I had made the concept of rule by divine right palatable by dint of their personal popularity and their skill in working with Parliament. Not so the Stuarts. James I was a Scotsman, a foreigner, never really taken to their hearts by the people. His son Charles was somewhat more popular, but he could see no necessity for foregoing the perquisites of the throne to make realistic compromises with Parliament. Both James and Charles tried to steer in the direction of absolute monarchism by divine right; Parliament strove with equal conviction to take unto itself ultimate legislative and administrative authority. Strands of religious conflict were threaded through it all—high-church leanings versus low-church tenets, supported by various other Protestant sects, later including the extremist elements of Puritanism.

From 1629 to 1640 Charles ruled without Parliament. During those 11 years his subjects were busily engaged in choosing sides for what would be called the "Great Rebellion." In 1640 Parliament was reconvened and demonstrated at once that 11 years of enforced idleness had not cooled its recalcitrance. In 1642 Charles ordered the arrest of five of his chief opponents in the House of Commons. They evaded arrest, Charles went north to rally armed support, Parliament assumed the reins of government, and armed conflict swept the country.

Peace was not restored for seven years. The fortunes of war swayed from side to side until a Puritan named Cromwell assumed a decisive role by defeating the king's forces at Naseby in 1645. From that point all Charles' fortunes were downhill, culminating in his capture by Cromwell in 1649. He was brought before the "Rump" Parliament—so-called because all likely royal sympathizers were excluded by force of arms—and there ordered to be tried before a special high court. He was condemned to death and, on January 31, 1649, beheaded. The Stuart line was still preserved, how-

ever, in the person of his son Charles, safe in France.

The Commonwealth lasted from 1649 to 1660. Their king gone, the English now found themselves a republic, with Cromwell the dominant figure. The Rump Parliament continued right on into the Commonwealth and proved to be thoroughly unresponsive to suggestions that its membership be enlarged and its radical procedures moderated. Finally its dissolution was accomplished by the same tactics that had reduced it to rump dimensions in the first place—force of arms. In December of that year, 1653, Cromwell set himself up as Lord Protector of the Commonwealth.

With the advent of the Commonwealth the somber pall of Puritan austerity soon fell upon the land. Frowned upon were the laces and embroideries once lavished upon costume for men and women alike. Puritan dress became exceedingly plain. Rules against horse-racing, cock-fighting, dog-baiting, bear-beating, gambling, the theater, fireworks, public dancing and all manner of frivolous amusements bore the imprint of sober, earnest persons determined upon strict compliance. Historian Thomas Macaulay commented wryly that bear-baiting was prohibited not because it gave pain to the bear but because it pleasured the spectators.

This period saw the beginning of a great national addiction: tea-drinking. Tea was introduced into England during the mid-1650's and reportedly

was first offered for sale at Garway's Coffee House in London in 1657. There are no evidences of tea-flowers, however, in crewel embroideries.

Embroidering appeared not to lose favor, but the gaiety of it seemed to have departed. Stump work and petitpoint pictures were then much the fashion, often with Old Testament themes. Ladies of royalist sympathies clothed their embroidered figures in styles suggesting Charles I and his queen, but there was little real spirit in this kind of needlework.

However, not even Puritan gloom could quite quench the derisive humor of the people. Some while before Cromwell dissolved Parliament, the people, wearying of its antics, bestowed upon it a name of their devising—Barebone's Parliament. This name was derived from an obscure member, a London leather-seller and sometime preacher named Barebone Barbon. His fervent shoutings from the pulpit earned him the sobriquet "Praise-God Barebone."

Derisive, too, was this barbed verse of the time:

> "To Banbury came I, O profane one,
> Where I saw a Puritane-one,
> Hanging of his cat on Monday
> For killing of a mouse on Sunday."

Oliver Cromwell died in 1658, and the mantle of Lord Protector fell upon his son Richard. The strength of the father did not likewise fall with the mantle, and soon the reins of government were in the hands of army leaders. In an attempt to end the recurring political upheavals Parliament was called back into session and, prompted by the Army, offered the crown to Charles Stuart, then residing in France. He returned to England as Charles II, and so began the merry period known as "The Restoration."

Charles II (1660-1685) was only 11 when his life of adventure began. Before he was 21 he had seen military action with his father in the north of England; he had been required to join his mother in France after the defeat at Naseby; he had participated in an unsuccessful Holland-based attempt to make an armed landing in England; he had sent Parliament a signed and sealed carte blanche upon which to impose any terms it wished in exchange for his father's life (an offer spurned by Parliament); and, after his father's death, he had made his way to Scotland and was there crowned king on New Year's Day, 1651, five months before his 21st birthday.

Shortly thereafter he gathered an army for invasion of England and was roundly defeated by Cromwell. He had no option but flight. Disguised as a simple country fellow, he made his way for five weeks through the English countryside, hoping to reach the sea and safety in France. His flight through England, especially a day spent hiding in an oak tree while his enemies scoured the country thereabouts—captured the imagination of vicarious adventurers. It also gave acorns and oak leaves a new significance to those of Stuart inclinations.

The next few years were for Charles ones of precarious existence, haunted by perpetual lack of funds and buffetings from country to country as Cromwell's displeasure was made manifest toward those who granted him asylum. Through it all, however, he was cheerful, tolerant and generous and seemed to have the faculty of not allowing the cares of tomorrow turn to ashes the pleasures of today. When he returned to England as Charles II he had a well-developed appreciation of the gay, the lively, the pleasurable and the colorful.

The country lost no time in saluting his return. Scenes of wild rejoicing, flower-strewn roads, church bells, houses decorated with all manner of colorful hangings, thundering cannon, wine-filled fountains, milling, churning, shouting thousands accompanied his retinue every step of the way to the palace. Ten long years of restraints upon normal inclinations toward pleasure, of a morass of prohibitions, taboos and interdicts, burst free in a single glorious day—and kept on bursting.

Interest in embroidery revived. Stump work was still highly regarded, but now it was crewel work which had caught the public fancy. Upholstered furniture had been introduced to England, and with it there was a diminished need for chair, stool and bench coverings. Embroidery for costume was no longer popular, having been superseded by the profuse use of laces and ribbons. The most fashionable pieces for the industrious—and the ambitious—were now bed hangings, curtains and valances.

Activity on these was launched with great enthusiasm, with twilled linens used for the backgrounds and wool yarns used to fill in the designs. The repertoire of stitches, while not nearly so extensive as in the case of the earlier works, was now more effectively used. Shadings were subtler, largely due to the knowledgeable employment of the versatile long and short stitches. Other popular stitches included coral, stem, herringbone and knots. Some or all of these are to be found in most of the pieces of this period. Perhaps the very size of these undertakings dictated the obvious advantage of time-saving in the disciplined use of five or six stitches as against less certain handling of 15 or 20. The range of colors was, for some reason, somewhat curtailed also. Monochromatic color schemes were often used. Greens in many shadings and reds in many shadings appear to have been the most favored colors of the time.

Patterns in vogue during this era can be grouped into two broad classifications: (1) designs flowing from earlier English inspirations—coiling tendrils, branches, trees, fern and feather patterns; and (2) an "exotic" group, with variations on the "Tree of Life" theme, large stems and trees arising from hillocks, large coiled acanthus-like leaves, occasional highly imaginative flowers and animals,

A wealth of flowers, foliage, exotic birds and animals and a "Tree of Life" form a rich design on this English crewel-work panel, embroidered on twill-woven linen and cotton and inscribed "Began Nov 3 1701 MM." *Courtesy Colonial Williamsburg, Williamsburg, Va.*

natural or exotic. Of the two, the latter were most favored by embroiderers of the late seventeenth century.

It is interesting to compare what would seem to be modern lineal descendants of late-seventeenth-century pieces in design, coloring and stitchery.

The outstanding characteristics of crewel embroideries of this period are: large curtains worked on twilled linen; bold designs incorporating intertwined branches or stems, large curled leaves with notched edges, exotic flowers and, to a lesser degree, exotic animals; the recurring Tree of Life theme, with fern-like foliage; a restrained use of color, with much monochrome; compactly filled backgrounds; simple stitches.

The description of the Abigail Pett curtain, (on the next page), supplied by the Victoria and Albert Museum shows the typical stitches and colors of the period:

"Wool on cotton and linen, twill weave; long and short, split, stem, satin, feather and herringbone stitches, with laid and couched work and cross-stitch fillings. Colours: indigo, dark blue-green, emerald, pale blue-green, yellow-green, yellow, orange-buff, yellow-brown, fawn, red-brown, sepia, chocolate, carmine. Irregular pattern of scattered tree motives in four uneven rows, six or seven motives to the row. . . . With the trees, which are mainly exotic, are grouped animals (camel, griffin, leopard and lion with pennon, two monkeys in a bush, running stag, squirrel in nut bush), birds (peacocks, stork with frog) and human figures (two morris dancers, man with flag, man with gun, fisherman). The trees are either on green-shaded hillock ground or on gnarled Chinese stems; their large leaves usually have dentated edges, the smaller are pointed or lobed. All are shaded to the tips in solid embroidery or with fancy laid work and cross-stitch fillings; the stems are shaded to one side in brown."

A legal legacy of the period, the act of habeas corpus, which was enacted in the midst of the stormy passions wracking England during the late 1670's, became a foundation stone in the structure of law shielding the people against oppression by the state. The people seemed to have returned to their normal preoccupations when Charles II let fall the reins of power to his brother in 1685.

James II (1685-1688) was on the scene but a short while, for his presence upon the throne loosed once again the passions which had but lately subsided. Within three years he abandoned the throne for sanctuary in France, and the crown was offered his daughter Mary, and her husband, William of Orange. Her consuming interest in embroidery drew this comment: "In all those hours that were not given to better employment, she wrought with her own hands; and sometimes with so constant a diligence as if she had been [forced] to earn her bread by it. It was a new thing and looked a sight to see a Queen work for so many hours a day."

William and Mary (1689-1702) presided over the final decade of a tumultous century during which there was a tremendous outpouring of fancy embroidery, a torrent of needlework, crested by boldly imaginative, lavishly executed designs in crewel. Yet crewel work, like the departing century, would soon be walking in the shadows. As the century drew to its close, silk once more began to capture public preference. One of the earliest manifestations of this impending change was a popular form of needlework used in upholstering chairs and settees which was a combination of wool and silk, with tent and cross stitches worked in colored crewels and silks on canvas.

Queen Anne (1702-1714) was also a daughter of James II and the last of the Stuarts. Members of the House of Hanover—Georges I, II, III and IV—were to follow her. A description of the royal apartments at Hampton Court during Queen Anne's reign by an energetic sightseer, Celia Fiennes, included her observation of a closet opening out of the Queen's dressing-room in which the hangings and the coverings of chairs and stools were of needlework designed with "beasts, birds, images and fruits" which had been stitched by the late Queen Mary and her ladies.

Part of a set of bed curtains and valances made in England in the second half of the seventeenth century by Abigail Pett, who embroidered her name in an oblong within a large leaf on one valance. *Courtesy Victoria & Albert Museum, London, England.*

(*Facing page*)

A detail from the Abigail Pett curtain, showing the variety of shading and filling stitches employed within a single unit. *Courtesy Victoria & Albert Museum, London, England.*

Flowing arboreal designs were popular motifs for bed hangings, as shown in this typical example, embroidered in England on a linen-and-cotton background about 1700. *Courtesy Cooper Union Museum for the Arts of Decoration, New York.*

(*This page, top*) Large curling leaves twining tendrils and pomegranates were combined with unusual flowers to form large-scale designs like this late-seventeenth-century example of English crewelwork, beautifully executed in shades of indigo. *Courtesy Cooper Union Museum for the Arts of Decoration, New York.*

(*This page, bottom*) Tree-trunks, characterized by effective use of brick stitches, and lavish foliage in deep, rich colors mark this English-made set of bed-hangings, now displayed in the Ashley House in Old Deerfield, Mass. *Courtesy Heritage Foundation, Deerfield, Mass.*

(*Facing page, top*) Elongated flowers and plumelike leaves joined by slender, curving stems were embroidered in a warm shade of light red wool yarn in this seventeenth-century English hanging. *Courtesy Cooper Union Museum for the Arts of Decoration, New York.*

(*Facing page, bottom*) Elements of earlier embroidery designs are often adaptable to modern interiors, such as the flowing, elongated leaf pattern used on this bedspread. *Embroidered by Mrs. Everett W. Moxon, Falmouth, Mass.*

Two sprays of leaves provide a related motif for this pair of curtains. *Embroidered by Mrs. Richard H. Sweet, Sullivan, N. H.*

The same leaf motif is used for a companion chair-seat. *Embroidered by Mrs. Theodore Bennett, Chestnut Hill, Mass.*

(*Facing page*)

Holly leaves and berries are embroidered in tones of green, brown and crimson on this set of English eighteenth-century twill bed-hangings. *Courtesy The Royal Ontario Museum, University of Toronto, Toronto, Can.*

Part of a valance from the same "holly" set. *Courtesy The Royal Ontario Museum, University of Toronto, Toronto, Can.*

(*This page, top*) An early-eighteenth-century quilted linen bedspread made in England features a polychrome floral design in a central medallion, a bouquet in each corner and single flowers and buds in a continuous border. The embroidery, mostly chain stitch, is very fine and precise. *Courtesy Royal Ontario Museum, University of Toronto, Toronto, Can.*

(*This page, right*) The quaint figures in this example may represent the Biblical figures of Adam and Eve. It was apparently done in 1704 by an English or American embroiderer. *Courtesy Heritage Foundation, Deerfield, Mass.*

(*Facing page, top*) Exceedingly fine stitches were employed by an eighteenth-century embroiderer to render the precise detail of this rather formal design (probably French), with its delicate birds, flowering shrubs, baskets of fruit, medallion and scrolled border. *Courtesy Museum of Fine Arts, Boston, Mass.*

(*Facing page, bottom*) Bands of embroidery were often used to trim skirts and petticoats. This panel of roses and thorns was embroidered in France during the first half of the eighteenth century. *Courtesy The Metropolitan Museum of Art, New York, Gift of Irwin Untermyer, 1954.*

Wool embroideries continued to decline in favor during the opening decade of the eighteenth century, but exotic motifs remained strongly in vogue. "Chinoiserie" was highly esteemed, and detached sprays or formal clusters of flowers began to supplant the flowing stem and branch motifs which until then had predominated in crewel work. Silk became the important medium, and with it came greater delicacy of line and improvement in shading techniques.

Once again costume embroidery became fashionable. About this time a complaint appeared in the *Spectator* (1714) that the young ladies of the day were a capricious, indolent, pleasure-seeking lot, coupled with a recommendation that "no virgin be allowed to receive the addresses of her first lover but in a suit of her own embroidering."

But crewel embroidery, a casualty to fashion's eternal restlessness, was not forgotten; it was to be safely transplanted by those who would carry its cherished traditions and techniques to the New World. The present upsurge of interest after so many years bears testimony to its timelessness.

By the time the eighteenth century opened many towns and hamlets had already sprung up in America along the Atlantic seaboard and the slopes of the range of mountains to the west. For the women who plied their needles to clothe their families and provide linens for their households, all that had been developed in generations past served as a model for their own "fancy work," yet each embroiderer found she had to adapt to new conditions, new circumstances.

The need to accommodate long-familiar ways to the demands of a bewildering new land faced the colonists, who sought to shape the wilderness as best they could in the likeness of their former homes. For many years utility and frugality went hand in hand. Objects had to be useful first, decorative second. Even if decoration could be added, materials for embroidery were scarce, expensive to import and costly in time and effort to make at home.

But colonial ingenuity was present in the construction of frames, in the making of cloth and, especially in the discovery and utilization of local dyestuffs. Recipes for vegetable dyes were undoubtedly included in the herbal lore handed down from mother to daughter. Friendly Indians may have added to this store of knowledge by showing the colonists how to use native plants— roots, berries, tree barks—to obtain a variety of usable colors. Indigo plants produced beautiful shades of blue, while yellowed wools responded to dipping in indigo by coming out in varying shades of blue-green. Goldenrod, broome sedge, sheep laurel, sumac and madder all contributed to the meager supply of ingredients available to the early colonists. A little later the quality and quantity of colors in the red family were augmented by cochineal (a dried tropical insect) and a dye extract from the tropical logwood tree (apparently from Brazil, and probably referring to the "brasell" color used in embroideries). Dyeing techniques were often worked out by trial and error, and successful combinations were closely-guarded household secrets.

Existing examples of colonial work show their embroiderers to have been exceptionally skilled in the use of color. Their colors are still pleasing—soft, harmonious, nicely shaded, with evidence of much dexterity in blending. Polychrome designs seemed generally favored, although the ready availability of indigo dyes encouraged the development of a blue-and-white embroidery tradition. The colonial housewife had the added inspiration of the lovely "blue Canton" chinaware then being introduced to the colonies by New England sailors returning from the Orient. Blue and white work, sometimes done in crewels, and sometimes in linen threads, attained some popularity in Colonial America, but is perhaps best known today as a result of its revival just at the close of the nineteenth century. Considering the handicaps under which they often had to work, colonial ladies, with their home-brewed dyes and homespun materials, did very well indeed.

Not too much information about stitchery in the

very early days is available. Adaptability to surface application was important when there was a scarcity of wool yarns, a chronic condition at first. During the later colonial period stitches were effectively used and not too elaborate. The most popular, as shown by those early pieces which have been preserved, were chain, buttonhole, herringbone, loop, outline, long and short, Rumanian, stem and satin. These examples also indicate a refreshing freedom in combining stitches.

Linen and woolen materials in the early years were undoubtedly made at home, where spinning and weaving were daily household chores. Later, imported materials became more abundant and the choice between imports or homespun depended on access to sources of supply and the ability to pay for costly imports. Those in modest circumstances had to rely largely upon their own resources while affluent citizens of seaport communities were probably content with nothing less than the latest and best from the fashion capitals of Europe.

At first the popular designs were largely in the English tradition, although the colonists had not the means nor materials to render them in any lavishness. In time the colonial housewife began to draw upon the local scene for new inspiration, and gradually a modified "American" tradition began to emerge. The familiar arboreal and floral motifs remained but were developed along somewhat simpler lines, with emphasis on economy of execution. They often seemed to convey a feeling of spaciousness, perhaps reflecting an environment where open country as far as the eye could see was a fact of life.

There is evidence that professional patterns were available, both those which could be imported from England and those developed by teachers of sewing and pattern-makers in the colonies. Similarity in the arrangement of motifs and in the way flowers and animals are depicted in a number of examples suggest a fairly wide currency for a few standard designs.

The individual embroiderer was also not without resources of her own in creating unique designs from themes familiar and dear to her. The Hall bedspead is an excellent example (following page 48). Delightfully conceived and colorfully wrought, the piece communicates at once a personal pleasure in a beloved flower garden and a desire to retain its warmth and charm during the long cold winter months. It is engagingly attractive, and thoroughly American.

The unicorns, griffins and other chimerical beasts occasionally found in English works seem to have excited no interest in the colonies and are seldom found. The colonists seemed to prefer animals of a gentler sort.

Surviving examples of crewel embroidery suggest that bed furnishings were one of the major concerns of the early American housewife. In those days, many fireplaces, warming pans and hot bricks, nightcaps, warm bed-coverings and hangings with which to enclose the beds against drafts were deemed essential to comfort. The bed was usually the most important piece of furniture in the house and, where means were at hand, the most lavishly decorated. Several kinds of bed-furnishings are illustrated, including a set now hanging in the Governor's Palace of the Williamsburg restoration. Also shown are a curtain believed to have been made in Ipswich, Massachusetts, between 1720 and 1750, a bedspread dated by its maker, Mary Breed, in 1770, a bedspread owned by the uncle of John Hancock and a bedspread made by Clarissa Stohart Deyo in Kingston, New York, in 1728.

The Ipswich curtain, attributed to the Wade family, is a delightful example of scattered floral and variegated leaf units. Composition, selection of colors and stitches, particularly those used for filling purposes, are all pleasing and effective. The stitches employed include chain, loop, seed, long and short, satin and stem. The Mary Breed spread, made by a resident of Boston, has an indigenous charm and shows a lively imagination. Both the bell-pull reproduction displayed in the Tryon Palace (N.C.) restoration and the modern panel featuring a single bird motif from the Mary Breed

(From left to right)

A workbag bordered in a floral design holds tightly twisted "sticks" of crewel yarns. It is displayed in the Hall Tavern, Old Deerfield, Mass. *Courtesy Heritage Foundation, Deerfield, Mass.*

A standing circular embroidery frame is displayed in the Ashley House, Old Deerfield, Mass. *Courtesy Heritage Foundation, Deerfield, Mass.*

Round embroidery frames were also designed so that they could be placed on the top of a table, chest or bureau. This frame is now in the Asa Stebbins House, Old Deerfield, Mass. *Courtesy Heritage Foundation, Deerfield, Mass.*

This embroidery frame with stand was fashioned from ash, cherry and pine in New York State about 1750-1755. Strands of crewel yarn and a partially completed design are shown on the frame. *Courtesy The Metropolitan Museum of Art, New York, Rogers Fund, 1940.*

spread are true progeny of this colonial master-piece.

Companion pieces of furniture were not neglected. Chair-coverings and seats, cases for pillows and cushions, tablecloths, fire screens and framed pictures were among the many everyday household items engaging the embroiderer's attention. Crewel work for costume was also favored. Petticoat panels sometimes portrayed animated scenes in gay colors, including trees, flowers, animals and figures. Gowns for women and children were often embroidered in crewel. Pocket aprons which held yarns, needles and other notions, pocketbooks, workbags and purses were among crewel-worked accessories. Often scraps of homespun linen were seamed together to make these. In concept and execution of all these articles a basic simplicity is apparent. Designs varied considerably but never wandered far from traditional flowers, wavy branches, stems and vines. Stitches were simple and effectively used. Popular ones included chain, satin, Rumanian and stem. In a class by themselves are the few crewel-embroidered wedding gowns of eighteenth-century vintage which have been preserved as outstanding examples of the highly imaginative use of embroidery in costume decoration.

Many museum pieces bear witness to a lively appreciation of the art of crewel, particularly in New England, but also in such areas as Pennsylvania, New York, New Jersey and Virginia.

By the end of the century styles in furniture had changed and elaborate bed hangings were no longer in vogue. Enthusiasm for crewel work gradually became submerged in the gentle contemplation of sweet sorrow which overcame the maidens of the new nation in the early 1800's. Memorial wreaths and scenes of romantic musings amid ruins or gardens seemed to best express the elegiac mood of the period. Even the word "crewel" was tucked away for a while.

A revival of interest in old-time ornamental needlework came in England about 1872. The Royal School of Art Needlework, established in South Kensington, sponsored the restoration and imitation of rare and elaborate specimens of antique embroidery to decorate wealthy homes and to provide employment for needy women. Both old and new needlework designs were exhibited at the Centennial Exhibition in Philadelphia in 1876, and soon similar classes were instituted in New York sponsored by the Society of Decorative Art.

This set of four linen seat covers, with a variety of figures, animals and floral motifs, was embroidered in Connecticut about 1730. The mounds, or hillocks, were a traditional feature in designs of this period. *Courtesy The Metropolitan Museum of Art, New York, Gift of Mrs. J. Insley Blair, 1946.*

42

(*Facing page, top*) A pine tree provides an interesting motif in this strip of a petticoat border, made in New England, probably Massachusetts, 1725-1750. *Courtesy Museum of Fine Arts, Boston, Mass.*

(*Facing page, center*) A squirrel sits in one flowering tree and a parrot in another, with various animals in the grass below, in another section of the petticoat border. *Courtesy Museum of Fine Arts, Boston, Mass.*

(*Facing page, bottom*) Still another section of the same petticoat border, with a clump of small pine trees and several animals. *Courtesy Museum of Fine Arts, Boston, Mass.*

(*Above*) A motif with flowers on drooping stems was selected by a New England embroiderer for this linen valance, probably made in Massachusetts, about 1750. *Courtesy Museum of Fine Arts, Boston, Mass.*

(*This page, top*) Mary Breed of Boston signed and dated (1770) her own crewel-embroidered linen bedspread, with its sprightly motifs—random sprays and clumps of flowers, small flowering trees and birds. She chose a color scheme of pink, blue, yellow and green. *Courtesy Metropolitan Museum of Art, New York, Rogers Fund, 1922.*

(*This page, bottom*) The quaint charm of the birds-in-a-flowering tree motif in the original Mary Breed bedspread has been retained in a simplified version. The branches of the tree have been spread open for an airier effect. *Courtesy Arthur H. Lee & Sons, Inc., New York and Birkenhead, England.*

(*Facing page, top*) Animals, flowers and fruit were worked simply in red wool on cotton, in outline, blanket and seed stitches, on this early-eighteenth-century bed curtain. *Courtesy The Metropolitan Museum of Art, New York, Rogers Fund, 1940.*

(*Facing page, bottom*) Plant and bird designs have been embroidered in shades of blue wool on these three eighteenth-century pieces. They are traditionally said to have been brought to Essex, Mass., by Madam Susanna, wife of Sylvester Eveleth. *Courtesy Essex Institute, Salem, Mass.*

44

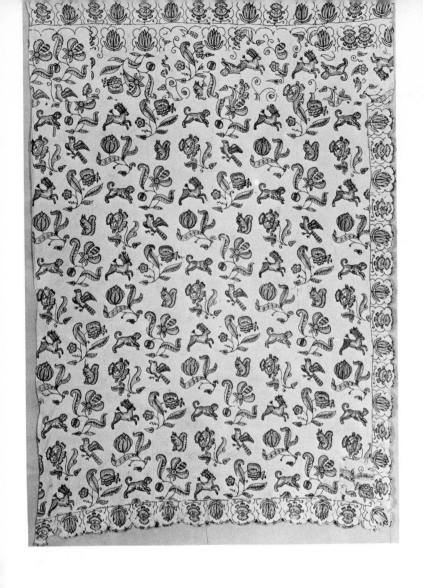

45

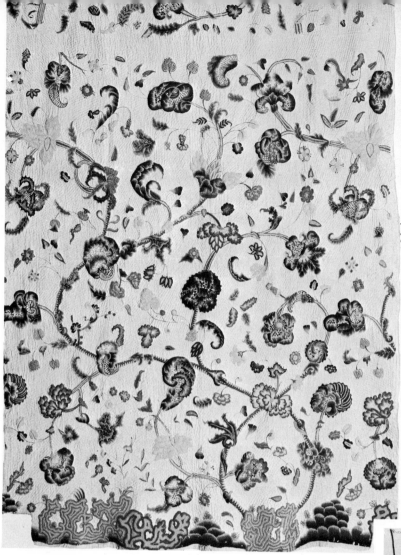

(*Above*) This American bedcover was made up in the nineteenth century from part of a set of bed curtains said to have been worked by Mrs. Richard Fifield of Boston, about 1712-1714 in crewel yarns on cotton-and-linen twill. *Courtesy Museum of Fine Arts, Boston, Mass.*

(*Right*) The arms of the Hancock family of Boston form the motif at the center bottom of the field of this white linen bedspread embroidered in crewels in shades of blue, green, rose, yellow and buff. The effect of trellis couching in the centers of some of the flowers has been achieved by means of outline stitches. The trellis work and scrolls are made of an applied blue-green woolen tape. According to tradition, it was originally owned by Thomas Hancock (1703-1764) and may have been made at the time of his marriage in 1730. The spread later belonged to his nephew and heir, the patriot John Hancock (1736-1793). *Courtesy Henry Francis du Pont Winterthur Museum, Winterthur, Del.*

Leaf sprays and flowers decorate a child's linen-and-cotton dress of the mid-eighteenth century. *Courtesy The Metropolitan Museum of Art, Rogers Fund, 1954.*

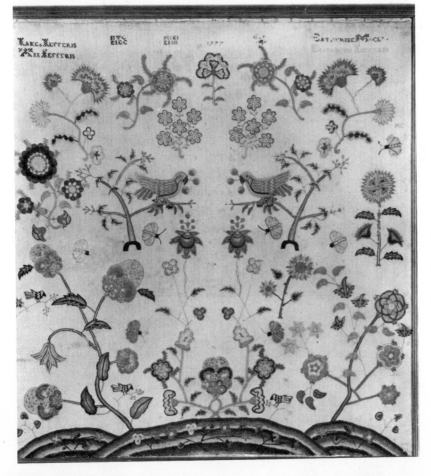

Elizabeth Jefferis of Pennsylvania worked this linen sampler in 1777 in pastel tones. Birds, butterflies and flowering shrubs spring from mounds to make an appealing composition, worked in long and short stitches and French knots. *Courtesy The Metropolitan Museum of Art, Rogers Fund, 1959.*

47

Crewels had not been manufactured for some years, but by the early 1880's there was some demand in America for worsted yarns once again. Flowers and vines in the style referred to as "grandmother's crewel work" were being embroidered on innumerable tidies, towels, valances, window shades, portieres, splash curtains for washstands, tea cloths, cushion covers, carriage covers, shoebags, workbags, aprons, screens and lambrequins (mantel-covers). Near the end of the nineteenth century a group of women in Deerfield, Mass., dedicated themselves to reviving such earlier arts as crewel embroidery. Their designs, generally done in blue and white, were worked both in worsted and in linen threads.

Occasional custom pieces of crewel embroidery were made by a few firms which specialized in this field for private and official residences, institutions, etc., but for a long time there was a decline of interest in time-consuming individual embroidery and little or no demand for crewel wools. Again manufacturers dropped them although they continued to offer the more popular silks and flosses.

Then, in the middle of the twentieth century, once again it became a household word. Like the greatly increased national interest in historic restorations, there seemed to be a groundswell of interest as the comfortable, easy-to-live-with designs reappeared.

Commenting on the widespread and knowledgeable interest in antiques and the arts of an earlier age, Nona B. Brown discussed the tide of visitors to Virginia's Williamsburg in *The New York Times*:

"It is no news that this age of mass production has had its own antithesis in the "do-it-yourself" trend. But is it not possible that some of this has sprung from a desire to keep alive, in available leisure time, the artistic craftsmanship of our own forebears? Or the desire to have finer, more individualized possessions? Or a combination of both?

Williamsburg itself has found or trained craftsmen who can do eighteenth-century work of all kinds. . . . Their work is magnificent. No wonder it is admired and leads a consuming public to want something similar, either authentically old or well copied by hand today.

The revival of popular interest in fine needlepoint embroidery started some time ago. *Now, the more difficut art of crewel embroidery is beginning to make a comeback.*"

As for the contemporary interpretation of this precious heritage, why should not today's embroideries stand proudly with the best? Our color values span the spectrum, we have materials in an abundance and of a quality unmatched before, our libraries have volume after volume on their shelves devoted to stitches old and new. We acknowledge a basic desire to make something of beauty with our hands that will express our own taste and individuality. Crewel embroidery may be taken up, begun and added to at will, put aside and picked up again. Modern embroiderers also have the priceless gift of leisure time—more spare hours than the colonial housewife or even the diligent Queen Mary ever envisioned.

The future of crewel embroidery may be another "checkerid" tale of flowering and eclipse. But, fortunately for us, the traditional techniques of this unique art have not been lost or forgotten, and we may study and enjoy, at our convenience, even duplicate or adapt if we like, all those charms which have made it indeed an ageless art and have caused so many generations before ours to value their crewel pieces as family heirlooms.

Crewel embroidery is now in your hands, one hand a legatee of generations past, the other a harbinger of generations to come. May you enjoy in full measure both your gifts—the one you receive from the past, the one you prepare for the future.

(*Right*) A leaf motif used in a wide curtain from the same set. *Courtesy Museum of Fine Arts, Boston, Mass.*

(*Below*) Two motifs from the narrow curtain shown in color at left demonstrate the variety of decorative stitches at the command of the colonial embroiderer. *Courtesy Museum of Fine Arts, Boston, Mass.*

CHAPTER TWO

BASIC WORKING MATERIALS

THE standard materials you will need for crewel embroidery include lengths of a durable background material, usually a pre-shrunk linen twill, upon which the design is traced and then worked in wool yarn; skeins of crewel, or worsted, yarn; crewel needles and an embroidery frame or hoop. Materials and transferring techniques will be discussed briefly below; color planning, stitches, design units, finishing and blocking will be discussed in subsequent chapters.

Crewel embroidery supplies* may not be readily available in all communities; if not obtainable in the needlework department of your local department store or yarn shop, you may wish to order supplies by mail.

* Inquiries about sources of supply of linen twill, wools, needles, patterns and all other crewel items may be addressed to: Crewel, P. O. Box 5, Chestnut Hill, Massachusetts.

Background Material

The most commonly preferred cloth is a sturdy, natural-colored linen twill similar to the unbleached linen or wool used by needlewomen of the seventeenth and eighteenth centuries for their embroidered bed-hangings, curtains, cushions, aprons, workbags, etc. Ideally suited for crewel work, it provides a neutral, unobtrusive background for any color scheme and wears extremely well.

The most satisfactory grade of linen twill is described as "straight" twill, weighing 8 to 9 ounces per square yard and with approximately 100 threads to the square inch. If at all possible, it is best to begin your venture into the art of crewel embroidery with such linen twill. After you are thoroughly familiar with it, you can try other materials, such as heavy round-thread linen, available in natural and shades of brown, green, blue, gold, rose and other hues appropriate to modern decor, or damask or satin-finish woolens which are close to twill in weight, weave and color. The weave should be firm and close in any material selected for the most satisfactory results.

Yarns

Crewel yarns are fine two-ply twisted worsted yarns. They are obtainable in many beautiful gradations of color, so that opportunities for varied color schemes are unlimited. English yarns are generally finer than American yarns and are preferred by those who enjoy doing fine work.

Having an assortment of yarns in many colors is one thing; having them coordinated and ready for immediate use is quite another. You will want them neatly arranged and sorted by color values. When sorting and arranging yarns, do so by daylight if at all possible. True color selection under artificial light is very difficult. However, you can do perfectly satisfactory needlework at night if you use yarns previously selected in natural light. Your best stitch work will be done with yarn threads not over two feet long. Longer threads tangle easier, tend to become thin and drawn with repeated pulling and may become soiled from handling.

For an orderly arrangement of your yarns, take a piece of material approximately 14 inches wide by 36 inches long and, with a piece of 1-inch-wide tape, make a series of loops about 1 inch wide down the center to accommodate the number of values needed for your embroidery. When completed, insert your yarns arranged by value sequences from 1 to 5. If "value sequences" is an unfamiliar term to you, you may find it helpful to turn to the discussion of color values in the following chapter (page 57).

Unrolled, this yarn kit will spread your working colors before you, assembled and ready for immediate selection. Rolled up, it can be tucked away with the assurance that, upon taking it out again, your yarns will not have become dislodged or entangled.

Needles

Crewel needles, which are slightly shorter and have larger eyes than ordinary embroidery needles, have been developed to meet the exact requirements of this fine art, and you simply cannot do excellent work without them. They come in various sizes, but these three varieties are especially recommended:

ROLL UP YARN KIT

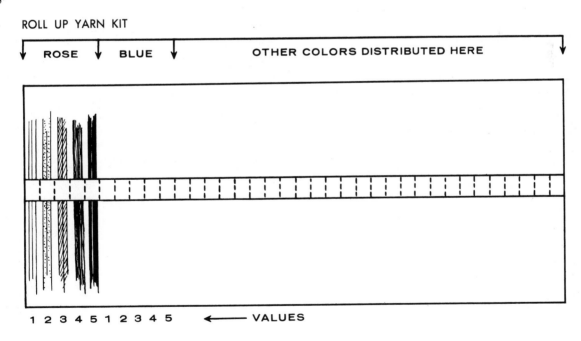

ROSE   BLUE   OTHER COLORS DISTRIBUTED HERE

1 2 3 4 5 1 2 3 4 5 ←——— VALUES

#3: This is a large needle for use when a double yarn strand is required.

#4: This is the indispensable tool, since it is used about 90% of the time in crewel embroidery. Always keep a small supply on hand.

#5: This is a much finer needle, not used often but extremely helpful when needed.

In addition to these, it is a good idea to have a tapestry needle available. This blunt-pointed needle is ideal for some forms of couching and interlacing stitches.

If you have not previously worked in wool yarns with a needle you may experience some difficulty in threading it. Loop the yarn around the needle shaft and pull it tight against the shaft. Next, grasp the loop and the needle (both together) firmly between thumb and index finger so the tip of the loop barely shows between the fingertips. Withdraw the needle without loosening your grip on the yarn and then press the eye of the needle down onto the yarn loop. The holding fingers will help groove the needle eye over the yarn, and there you have it. If this is too difficult a chore, try using a needle-threader. You have a thimble, of course.

Hoop or Frame

Before the expandable embroidery hoop was developed most crewel embroiderers used a standing frame. While the standing frame (somewhat similar to a rug-hooking frame) is still in use, the small expandable embroidery hoop has several advantages. It is a more flexible device, it can be carried about quite easily (and what woman doesn't want to take her embroidery with her at times?), it is readily available, in both wood and metal, in almost any department or variety store, and it is quite inexpensive.

So, choose a frame or hoop as you wish, but do use one or the other. You simply cannot do really fine work without having the material held tautly in place while working upon it. Taut material will minimize puckering, and it will be a great help in keeping your stitches uniform.

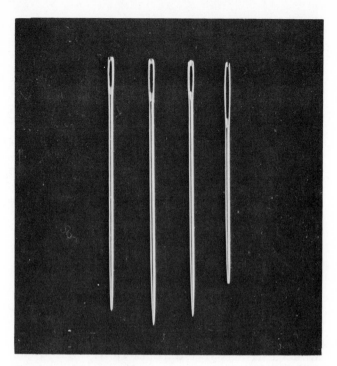

Crewel needles are approximately 1¾" long, with a long, slender eye. Shown here are #3, #4 and #5 crewel needles and a tapestry needle. *Photograph by Eddowes Co., Inc. Needles courtesy William Briggs and Company, Ltd., Manchester, England.*

An expandable embroidery hoop. *Courtesy D. M. C Corporation, New York.*

TRACING AND ENLARGING PATTERNS

There are various procedures by which a pattern may be prepared for embroidery upon a background material. In the interest of simplicity, however, only the most common techniques will be discussed here. But first, a word of caution. Be sure to allow ample cloth margins all around your pattern. Like the unfortunate man who spent all winter building a boat in his basement but found he could not get it out through the door, you may be crushed to complete the loveliest chair-seat only to discover that there is not enough margin material for proper upholstering. Don't let this happen to you!

Transfer Patterns

A wide variety of commercial transfer patterns is now available. It is a simple matter to iron such a tissue-paper pattern onto a square of material. Instructions are usually included, but in case you have mislaid them, here is what you do. First, be sure to cut away anything, such as manufacturer's name, serial number, etc., that is not a part of the pattern itself. You do not want these markings to show on your material. Next, spread the material smoothly over a flat surface *right side up*. Now, lay the transfer pattern smoothly over the material *shiny side down*. Center it carefully—remember those margins! With a very hot iron, go slowly and carefully over the whole pattern. Before removing the pattern lift one corner gently to check the depth of the impression on the material. If the design seems too light, repeat the ironing process until the lines are clear and easy to follow.

Tracing Your Own Designs

Outside the mainstream of regular transfer patterns thousands of other usable designs also abound. Down through the centuries imaginative embroiderers have evolved an infinite variety of design combinations based on the recurring motifs of crewel embroidery. Many of these are readily available, but often the design must first be copied and then transferred to cloth. This represents considerably more effort than merely ironing on ready-made transfer patterns, but it opens up a whole new vista of creative design and is one of the many personal delights of crewel embroidery.

Materials needed for tracing or adapting your own embroidery designs are:

1] Tracing paper. Use a good-quality paper embodying both strength and transparency. Thin architects' linen is a little more expensive but very good.
2] Carbon paper. A good-quality intense black carbon with a medium- to hard-finish will give a sharp reproduction with little or no smudging. Various types of coated or treated carbons now on the market are very good. If your background material is dark-colored, use a white carbon paper.
3] A medium-hard pencil (#3 is generally satisfactory).
4] A fine-point laundry-marking pen, with black or blue ink. Available almost everywhere at a nominal cost.

Copying Designs

In order to embroider your first piece of crewel you will soon be transferring a simple design from a page in this book onto a square of cloth. Perhaps, as your skill increases, you will find inspiration elsewhere and wish to adapt a design or a detail from another source. Here is the transfer procedure:

First, lay a piece of tracing paper or architects' linen over the design and, with your medium-hard pencil, trace the outlines. Do not bear down too heavily if you wish to avoid leaving grooves on the pages of the book. You can always go over the outline later with a pen if necessary.

Now, spread the background material smoothly over a flat surface *right side up*, then lay the newly-traced design over the material—and do remember those margins. Anchor the design firmly to the material with straight pins. Before pinning down the design completely slip the carbon paper between the design and the material, keeping the *carbon side down* on the cloth. Use as many sheets of carbon as required to underlie the entire pattern.

You are now ready to trace the design onto the cloth. Just how hard to bear down depends upon the type and color of the background material, the carbon paper utilized, the firmness of the working surface, etc. You may have to experiment a little to find out just which combinations work best for you.

As a final step, it might be a good idea to go over the design on the cloth with a laundry-marking pen in order to darken it indelibly. Do not be unduly concerned if your traced design perhaps bears a few random smudges. Your finished embroidery will cover much of it and the rest will be washed out in the final processing of the completed piece.

Reversing a Design

Whenever you wish to reverse the position of a design—for example, to show a flower face turning to the right instead of to the left—simply trace it on transparent paper and then turn the paper over. From the reverse side you can readily trace the flower onto the background material.

Enlarging or Reducing a Design

There may be a time when you would like to use a particular design that is ideal for a special piece you wish to make, except that it is only half as large as the space you wish to cover. Or, conversely, it may be too big and you may want to make it smaller. If you have had training in freehand drawing, this will probably pose no problem. Most of us, however, need a guiding hand to achieve satisfactory results. Some suggested methods are enlargement-by-squares, by diagonals and rectangles or by mechanical means such as photostatic enlargement.

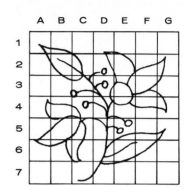

From left to right

Enlargement by Squares, Step 1.

Enlargement by Squares, Step 2.

Enlargement by Diagonals and Rectangles, Steps 1 and 2. *Courtesy The Studio Publications, London and New York.* Designing a Book Jacket, *Peter Curl.*

The Enlargement-by-Squares Method

First, draw a block of identical small squares over the original design, being careful to do them accurately. If the design is drawn or printed in black, which is likely, it would be wise to draw the squares in a contrasting color such as red or green. This will reduce the possibility of confusing lines of the design itself with those of the overlying squares.

Next, on a fresh sheet of paper draw a larger block with the *same number of squares*. This block must be large enough to cover the space available for the enlarged design. Now, duplicate each element of the design, square by square, in the large block of squares you have just made. Working carefully from one square to another, even a novice can execute an acceptable enlargement. If your first try is not quite as professional as you would like, your second effort undoubtedly will be an improvement.

This method is illustrated, along with an alternate one. The original floral design at the top has a covering block of 49 squares—seven rows of seven squares each. The enlargement below is drawn in a larger block of 49 squares made up of seven rows

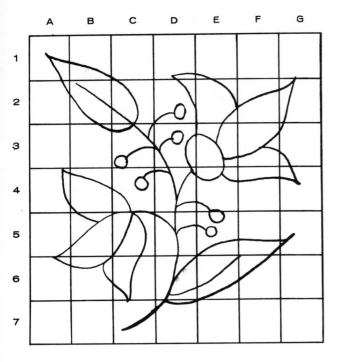

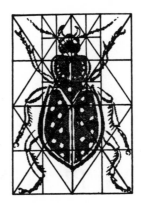

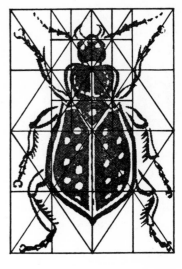

of seven squares each. Of course blocks of squares will not invariably work out to dimensions of 7 × 7. A long narrow design may require a block consisting of three rows of eight squares each. Use combinations of squares best suited to the job at hand. As a guide, you may find it useful to number and letter the columns and rows of squares. This will minimize the likelihood of errors such as drawing a line into C-4 that should go into D-4.

If you do not wish to mar the original design by drawing directly upon it, draw the squares on a piece of transparent tracing paper and fasten them over the design with adhesive tape that can be removed easily without bringing some of the paper along with it. If you do not want to draw your own squares, you may wish to use lined graph paper which is available in a variety of sizes of squares and printed on both opaque and transparent stock.

Enlargement by Diagonals and Rectangles

When working from a design that is smaller than the desired size, another artist's technique that might prove helpful is a combination of diagonals and rectangles. This method is simply to divide the smaller drawing diagonally by pencil lines, then to draw a line horizontally and another vertically through the intersection of the diagonals. Each of the smaller rectangles thus formed can then be divided in the same way. For bare areas of the design, no further division will be required, but special attention can be given to the complex details in certain blocks. Breaking down those blocks and working from one block to another, the larger-scale version of the design can be worked out, as in the case of the enlargement of the insect, as illustrated, by just repeating each part of the design enclosed within intersecting lines.

To reduce the size of a design, the process must be reversed.

Photostatic Enlargement

Another method of reproduction involving a change in scale is generally available to those living in urban communities. Shops handling blueprints and photostats often have equipment to enlarge or reduce drawings. You may consider the nominal cost involved an excellent exchange for the amount of time required to adapt a design yourself.

CHAPTER THREE

COLOR PLANNING

AN INTRODUCTION

COLOR is admittedly a complex and elusive subject upon which the last word has not been written and probably never will. Even that master of words Robert Louis Stevenson had difficulty in describing a specific color to a friend in London. Writing from Samoa in 1892, he asked that some samples of wallpaper patterns be sent out to him for use in a room he described as "a sort of bed and sitting room, pretty large, lit on three sides . . . the colour in favor of its proprietor at present is a topazy yellow. But then with what colour to relieve it? I should rather like to see some patterns of unglossy —well, I'll be hanged if I can describe this red— it's not Turkish and it's not Roman and it's not Indian, but it seems to partake of the two last, and yet it can't be either of them because it ought to be able to go with vermilion. Ah, what a tangled web we weave—anyway, with what brains you have left choose me and send me some—many—patterns of this exact shade."

Contemporary selectors of wallpaper and shades of yarn have one great advantage over Stevenson: a color chart. The essentials of color handling in crewel embroidery need not be complex. Those with an inherent sense of color need only a guiding suggestion here and there; those with a less well developed perception of color would likely to be confused rather than helped by a technical analysis. So this discussion is intended to be as simple as possible.

A good beginning is to read these observations on color straight through to the end. It will not take very long. Undoubtedly, not everything will be fully absorbed immediately, but this initial preview of the whole subject will be helpful when you return to specific points for guidance in handling of color in your crewel embroidery.

Color Harmony and Color Balance

There are two major objectives in color planning: color harmony and color balance. In achieving color harmony a blending of colors is sought that will be pleasing to the eye. This applies to the effect of the whole as well as to individual colors which lie side by side. In color balance the objective is a pleasing distribution of colors, with a selective emphasis on two or three dominant colors.

Consider for a moment how one might color effectively a map of the United States. You would probably not want to concentrate all your brilliant reds, for instance, in one place or side-by-side such as in an area made up of Maryland, Virginia and North Carolina. Rather, you would find that a more effective arrangement would involve a symmetrical distribution of the red over a much greater area, by choosing, for example, such widely-spaced areas as Virginia, Oregon and Texas. If you were to draw connecting lines from state to state you would see that these would form a triangle. This "triangle theory" will be discussed later at greater length.

Color Range

In a simplified approach to color planning particularly suited to the requirements of crewel embroidery six basic colors are employed: red, yellow, blue, green, brown and purple. Each of these six colors expands into a number of related colors; the red family, for instance, also includes rose, rust, brick and many other shades. In crewel embroidery the subtle related colors are usually preferred for best effect. Thus, rose, rust, brick are in frequent demand, while just plain bright red is seldom used. Interestingly enough, the use of purple was once reserved for royalty only. Infrequently found in older crewel pieces, it is quite popular today.

Color Values

Every color varies in intensity from light to dark. These variations are defined as values and num-

bered from 1 (light) to 5 (dark). Thus Rust 1 is light, Rust 3, is medium and Rust 5 is dark. At this point you might turn to the color chart (following page 64) in which the most commonly used colors are arranged in five-value sequences.

Of course there can be many more than five variations between the lightest and darkest values of any color; an exceptionally keen eye may be able to distinguish a dozen. The five-value range has been used here for the practical reason that until substantial skill has been attained in color-blending this is just about the maximum number of values that can be handled comfortably. In crewel embroidery, values should be far enough apart in color intensity so that differences are immediately apparent yet close enough to permit subtle variations. Five values will handle both assignments nicely.

Some yarn manufacturers offer as many as eight or more values in their selection of colors. In such cases try to select five values which cover the spread evenly between light and dark. Do not necessarily accept the manufacturer's designation as to lightest and darkest; his lightest may be too close to white or his darkest too close to black. When your color sense is sharpened you may find it interesting and stimulating to work with as many as six or seven values. For the time being, however, it is best to concentrate within the five-value range. When selecting or arranging yarns remember to do so by daylight if at all possible, since artificial light may cause some variation.

Color Overtones in Stitches

Before discussing monochrome, color harmony and color balance techniques in more detail it should be mentioned in passing that stitches also have chromatic overtones. Certain colors seem more radiant when used in conjunction with some stitches than with others. This is a very elusive subject to capture on paper and perhaps, to some extent, exists chiefly in the eye of the beholder. Nonetheless, it is an interesting concept and may yield some captivating results.

MONOCHROME

Before attempting to handle several shades you may want to try monochrome: to work with several values of a single color. When only one color is used there is no problem of harmony; the only problem is selection of value sequences. Working with a monochrome scheme is a simple technique, yet if done well, most effective. Many fine early Jacobean pieces were done in monchrome.

If you are working in monochrome you will want to build your color scheme around three to five values of a color that has a particular appeal for you. Generally, crewel tradition suggests the use of muted tones, but if you feel an irresistible urge to splash a bit, don't stifle the impulse. But this may be as good a place as any to counsel that you do curb any premature impulse to launch into a large, highly-colored piece before you are well-grounded in fundamentals. Your large pieces will be around a long time and will afford more lasting pleasure if the color-planning is sound.

Working in monochrome can provide an interesting foundation for stitch-practice and for developing a subtle touch in blending color values. You cannot be a really good colorist without proficiency in monochrome, for the delicate blending of values is the essence of color subtlety. A crewel piece may be striking done in bold, stimulating colors or in the traditional soft, muted tones, but it cannot be truly satisfying aesthetically unless boldness and/or subtlety are handled with skill. Design I, which follows immediately, will provide an opportunity for you to polish your skills. Suggested value sequences are included with the instructions accompanying the design.

If this is your first reading of this section on color we suggest you might do well to continue the discussion of color theory, then return to this first design.

The complete design and a photograph of the finished piece are shown below. The piece shown in the photograph was done in four values of blue-green. On the two pages following the design are detailed drawings and notes referring to value sequences and stitches applicable to the individual units of this pattern. Most of the drawings of units have value and stitch indications marked directly on them.

Now, before you begin, just a few quick reminders:

In transferring this pattern onto your background material, please follow carefully the directions given on page 53.

When starting a new strand of yarn anchor it securely by making several tiny running stitches where they will later be covered by embroidery. Anchor the end of a strand of yarn by weaving it back and forth on the wrong side, being careful that none of it shows through. *Never* anchor yarns by knotting them!

Before embroidering a leaf or petal in satin stitches *be sure* to outline the leaf or petal first with small back stitches. This adds finish to the work. For similar reasons, it is best to outline a leaf or petal with small running stitches before doing buttonhole stitches.

Before the piece is ready for use it must be properly finished and blocked. Complete directions for this procedure are found on pages 216-217.

This design can be used as a decoration for a small handbag (as shown), framed as a single picture, duplicated for a pair of pictures, as an embroidery for a large pincushion or as an unusual motif for a large pocket on a dress, skirt or jacket.

Design I, as used for a decoration on a handbag.

DESIGN I

This first design employs thirteen stitches. These include four basic stitches plus nine others directly associated with them.

1] Loop plus Chain, Attached Fly, Detached Fly
2] Knot plus Buttonhole, Open Cretan, Closed Cretan
3] Running plus Satin
4] Back plus Outline, Seed

All of these individual stitches should be prac-

ticed until you can do them easily. For detailed instructions, refer to the photographs and diagrams of stitches (pages 74-109). The index will provide page references for detailed notes on each stitch used here.

In this monochrome design you will be working with four values of one color of your own selection. Before choosing a color you would do well to turn to the color chart (following page 64) and study the various colors arranged there in five-value sequences. This will give you an excellent panorama of the scope of colors available for this first venture.

DESIGN I

1. Scalloped edge of leaf in satin stitch, value #1. Other edge outlined by two rows of closely worked knot stitches, using values #2 and #3. Fill with small seed stitches in value #3.

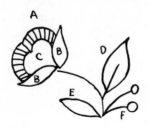

2. A. This band in satin stitch, value #2.
   B. Cretan stitches, closely worked, in value #3.
   C. Seed stitches in value #1.
   D. Use leaf E from Drawing 5.
   E. Satin stitch in value #2.
   F. Berries in small satin stitches, values #1 and #2; stems in outline stitch, value #3.

3. These little sprigs are attached fly stitches in value #2 and #3.

4. All tendrils are worked in knot stitches, value #2.

5. A. Top band in buttonhole, value #1; middle band in attached fly stitches, value #2; bottom band in satin stitches, value #3.
   B. Use F from Drawing 2.
   C. Satin stitch, value #2.
   D. Cretan stitch, value #3.
   E. Loop stitch in value #2.

6. A. The two bottom petals are filled solidly with chain stitches. Work the outside edges in value #4, the inside edges in value #1, then fill between with values #2 and #3 as shown.

   B. These two petals are edged with two rows of outline stitches, value #1 outside, value #2 inside. Complete with detached fly stitches in value #3.

   C. Stems of stamens in outline stitch, value #1; tips in satin stitches, value #2.

   D. Tendril done in knot stitch, value #2.

   E. Lower half of leaf in satin stitches, value #3; upper half edged with one row of chain stitches, value #2. Fill with small seed stitches in value #3.

7. A. This turned-over portion of the leaf is filled solidly with knot stitches. Place one or two rows in value #1 along the scalloped edge, then work the opposite edge in value #4. Between these rows fill with values #2 and #3, as shown.

   B. Edge this portion of the leaf with one row of chain stitches, using value #3.

   C. Small running stitches in value #2.

   D. Small seed stitches in value #3.

   E. For the stem use several (six or seven) rows of outline stitches with values #1 and #3 outside, value #2 in the center.

   F. Left half of this leaf to be filled with outline stitches, working from the edge to the center, using values #1, #2, #3, and #4 consecutively. Now, edge the other half of the leaf in one row of chain stitches in value #2, and fill with tiny seed stitches in value #3.

   G. Outline this leaf with chain stitches in value #3, then fill with open Cretan stitches worked into the chain stitches, using value #2. (Study the photograph showing completed design.)

   H. Satin stitch in value #3 for one-half of leaf; buttonhole stitch in value #4 for other half.

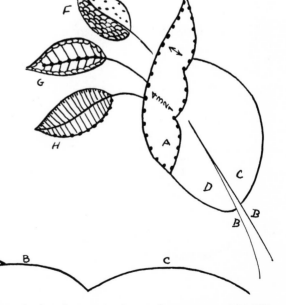

8. Mound A: Outline with three rows of outline stitches in values #1, #2 and #3, working from top down. Fill with seed stitches in value #4.

   Mounds B: Outline with two rows of knot stitches in values #2 and #3, working from top down. Fill with seed stitches in value #3.

   Mounds C: Outline with two rows of chain stitches in values #3 and #4, working from top down. Fill with seed stitches in value #4.

Note: For further discussion of mounds, see pages 136-138.

COLOR HARMONY

One of the harmonic peculiarities noted in crewel embroidery is the presence of muted greens in so many designs. Greens, so much a living part of the floral universe, are ever-present in the luxuriant vines, leaves, stems and shrubs of crewel embroidery.

This natural preponderance often places soft, muted greens in the role of background colors, leaving the dominant color roles to be played out by members of the red, yellow, blue, brown and purple families. Therefore, the major harmony problems usually revolve around pleasing combinations of colors from these five families. The brighter greens are most frequently used as accent or contrast colors.

One of the most effective ways to gain practice in applying the principles of color planning is to use colored pencils to "play around" with different color combinations on your paper pattern. Play it lightly, for your first choices may not be your final ones. So, sketch in short lines or small circles here and there, arranging and rearranging until the color combinations please you. Experimenting with colored pencils will aid you in establishing good color harmony and color balance.

When you feel your color arrangements are final you might find it reassuring to make a clean copy of the design and color it in completely. If you still like it, you are now ready to go ahead with confidence.

Contrasting, Accent and Dominant Colors

Contrasting colors, accent colors and dominant colors are three descriptive phrases you will encounter many times in this book.

PITMAN

Harmonious Combinations

First Color	Contrasting Colors
Blue—Old Blue	Gold—Rose
Aqua Blue	Old Gold—Rose
Chocolate Brown	Blue—Green
Golden Brown	Aqua Blue—Blue—Greens
Gold	Blue—Rose
Old Gold	Aqua Blue—Brick
Green—Blue Green	Gold—Rose
Aqua Green	Brick—Old Gold
Bright Green	Blue—Brick—Rose—Rust
Bright Yellow Green	Aqua Blue—Rust
Olive Green	Aqua Blue—Brick
Khaki	Aqua Blue—Blue—Rust
Purple	Old Gold—Rust
Rose—Strawberry	Blue—Gold
Rust	Aqua Blue—Gold
Brick	Blue—Old Gold
Strawberry	Blue—Gold

Grey is a neutral color and contrasts well with almost any color.

Harmonious Combinations

First Color	Accent Colors
Blue	Bright Green—Purple
Aqua Blue—Old Blue	Bright Yellow Green— Golden Brown— Chocolate Brown
Chocolate Brown	Gold—Rose
Golden Brown	Old Gold—Rust
Gold—Old Gold	Bright Green—Purple
Green	Blue—Golden Brown— Chocolate Brown
Aqua Green	Blue—Bright Yellow Green
Blue Green	Golden Brown—Chocolate Brown—Purple
Bright Green	Golden Brown—Chocolate Brown—Gold
Bright Yellow Green	Golden Brown—Chocolate Brown—Purple
Olive Green	Gold—Golden Brown
Khaki	Bright Yellow Green— Gold
Purple	Blue—Bright Green
Rose	Golden Brown—Chocolate Brown—Bright Green
Rust—Brick	Golden Brown—Chocolate Brown—Bright Yellow Green
Strawberry	Bright Yellow Green

Grey is a neutral color and will accept almost anything as an accent.

Contrasting colors are chromatic opposites which, when used together, tend to enhance each other. Old blue and gold are good examples. Old blue is quiet, somewhat dull, while gold is bright. When allied, they seem to take on a pleasant aura from each other. Contrasting colors are often used in approximately equal quantities. They are usually paired in approximately the same values: #1 against #1 or #2, or perhaps #4 against #3 or #5, but rarely #1 against #5.

Accent colors are used in crewel embroidery to enhance the chromatic appeal of quiet, unobtrusive colors. As a general rule, accent colors are bright, gay colors which create their most attractive effects when used sparingly. Just a few touches of rose or gold in muted green leaves, for example, give them life and make them much more interesting. Accent-color values are normally most effective in the #3–#5 range.

Dominant colors are just what the name implies: the most prominent colors in a design. Dominant colors will be discussed at greater length in the section following, entitled "Color Balance."

Here are two lists of suggested contrasting and accent colors based upon the color chart. They do not by any means exhaust all the various blending possibilities.

Before going on to discuss the color chart, one more general observation should be made about color selections for your embroidery: If you have any reservation about color choices in your first few pieces, take refuge in the softer, muted tones. Work up to bold colors after you have developed a "feel" for color mixing. Pieces with overly strong color schemes can become very tiresome—sometimes rather quickly.

Color Chart

The following color chart offers a representative grouping of the colors found most often in crewel embroidery. With them you can work almost any color magic you wish. These are by no means, however, all the color variations available in worsted yarns. A full display of *all* the minute color gradations available in yarn might well delight the most avid chromaddict—and leave just about everybody else floundering in a sea of colors. You may not always be able to obtain yarn in the shades precisely matching those on the chart. If not, use the closest matching colors obtainable if they are pleasing to you.

The colors on this chart have been identified by name for practical purposes of color keying. However, when you need yarns it is best to shop for them in person if possible. This is particularly true when attempting to match yarns already worked into a design.

With one exception—grey—each color on this chart has been divided into five values, with each value identified by number. Thus, whenever value #3 blue green, for instance, is referred to in any set of directions you can readily identify the exact color indicated.

The color arrangement is not accidental. The colors are arranged harmonically by rows, and row-by-row comments on these colors, their uses, their harmonic companions, their contrast and accent roles and related matters will be found on the page facing the chart.

COLOR BALANCE

A major objective in successful color planning is attainment of a balanced distribution of the colors used. In any combination of colors, deliberate or random, some will stand out more prominently than others. They may dominate because of their sheer chromatic strength or because they are used in sizable quantities, but in any case some colors, called dominant colors, inevitably stand out above others. Color balance seeks to use this fact to the best possible advantage. The observations made below have been generally geared to the role of dominant colors.

An elementary rule for color balance is simply: Never use any color in just one place in a design. When you have gained competence in balancing dominant colors, the handling of subordinate colors should pose no problems. Color balance is generally achieved by (1) an even distribution of approximately equal quantities of color all over a design, and (2) a symmetrical distribution of "islands" of color over the design; that is, application of what is known as the "triangle rule." The latter technique is used most frequently in crewel embroidery designs. There are, of course, almost unlimited variations of these two approaches.

Even Distribution of Color

An even distribution of approximately equal quantities of a color is one that is applied to a pattern with small open-faced flowers scattered more or less uniformly over it. This precise sort of treatment should be limited to smaller patterns, for in large designs it could easily become monotonous. A rigidly monotonous example of balance by even distribution is a checkerboard—an equal number of identical squares of alternating colors evenly distributed over the board. Fortunately, crewel embroidery designs do not come in such regimented patterns!

Balance by even distribution comes almost automatically in the use of repeat designs similar to those on pages 112-113. These small oblong designs are normally used in even-paced repetition and this rhythm in itself provides a balanced distribution. In a similar manner, large rectangular designs made up of symmetrical repetitions of one or two motifs practically carry built-in color balance.

Favorite flowers from Elizabethan gardens have been adapted to a set of curtains for a contemporary room. The pattern is called "Muncaster." *Courtesy Arthur H. Lee & Sons, Inc., New York and Birkenhead, England.*

This unusual piece of crewel embroidery was found in Pennsylvania. It is believed to be of European origin. *Photograph by Samuel Chamberlain. Courtesy of Heritage Foundation, Deerfield, Mass.*

This bedspread embroidered in dark multicolored wools on white linen by Clarissa Stohart Deyo in Kingston, New York, in 1728 is an example of Hudson River Valley needlework. *Courtesy Colonial Williamsburg, Williamsburg, Va.*

Some of the elements in the original Mary Breed bedspread of 1770—birds, cherries, thistles, etc.—were combined to form a vertical panel for a coral, blue and rose bellpull, which was embroidered in Birkenhead, England, by Arthur H. Lee & Sons, Inc., and which now hangs in the Daughter's Closet of the Tryon Palace Restoration in New Bern, N. C. *Courtesy Tryon Palace Restoration, New Bern, N. C.* (See also page 44.)

Cover for a chair-seat, embroidered in crewels on cotton-and-linen twill, in Massachusetts, 1700-1725. *Courtesy Museum of Fine Arts, Boston, Mass.*

Rich crewel-embroidered curtains and bed-hangings made in England may be seen with the furniture of the period during which they were originally used in the bedroom of the Governor's Palace in Williamsburg, Va. *Photograph by John Crane. Courtesy Colonial Williamsburg, Williamsburg, Va.*

An arrangement designed and embroidered by the author. *Color photograph by Bela Kalman.*

Detail of tree-trunk, from arrangement designed and embroidered by the author. *Color photograph by Bela Kalman.*

Mrs. Lucretia Hall of Charlemont, Mass., is said to have based the design for her varicolored and black bedspread on flowers which grew in her own garden. She is also reported to have carded and dyed the wool from her own sheep. The spread, believed to have been embroidered by Mrs. Hall about 1760-1770, is now in the Hall Tavern, Old Deerfield, Mass. *Photograph by Samuel Chamberlain. Courtesy Heritage Foundation, Deerfield, Mass.*

(*Facing page*) This narrow linen curtain, embroidered with crewels, is from a set of bed hangings believed to have been worked by a member or members of the Wade family of Ipswich, Mass., probably between 1725 and 1750. The stitches used were outline, stem, bullion, satin, chain, seed and long and short. *Photograph by Bela Kalman. Courtesy Museum of Fine Arts, Boston, Mass.*

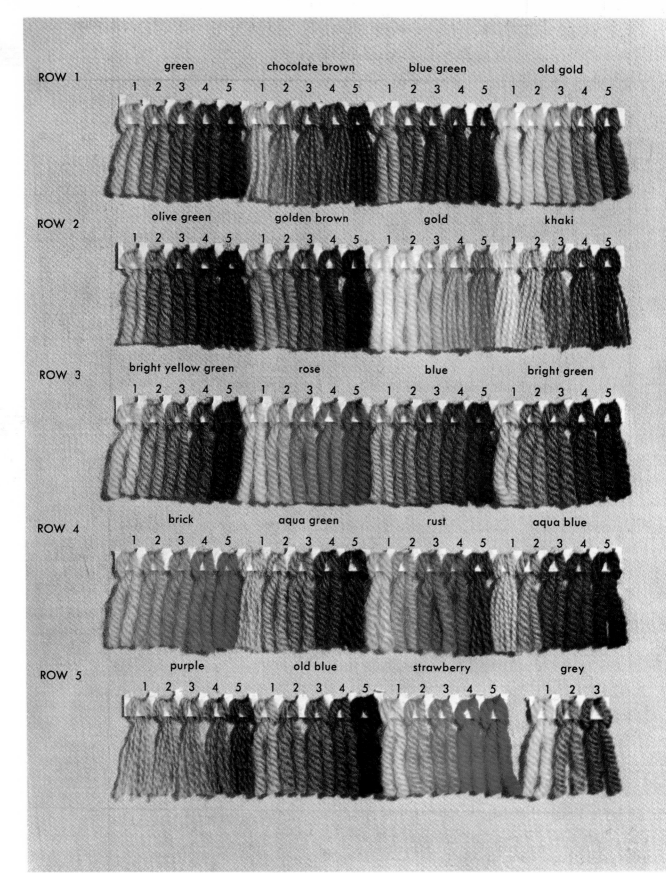

ROW 1
green   chocolate brown   blue green   old gold
1 2 3 4 5   1 2 3 4 5   1 2 3 4 5   1 2 3 4 5

ROW 2
olive green   golden brown   gold   khaki
1 2 3 4 5   1 2 3 4 5   1 2 3 4 5   1 2 3 4 5

ROW 3
bright yellow green   rose   blue   bright green
1 2 3 4 5   1 2 3 4 5   1 2 3 4 5   1 2 3 4 5

ROW 4
brick   aqua green   rust   aqua blue
1 2 3 4 5   1 2 3 4 5   1 2 3 4 5   1 2 3 4 5

ROW 5
purple   old blue   strawberry   grey
1 2 3 4 5   1 2 3 4 5   1 2 3 4 5   1 2 3

Color photograph by Bela Kalman.

COLOR CHART

Row 1: Green*, chocolate brown, blue green, old gold

These colors are all harmonious, and any two, any three, or all four of them may be used together in a pattern. They are particularly appropriate for large stems, branches and tree trunks. When so employed they may be used in approximately equal quantities, except for old gold, which is used chiefly for contrast or accent. The aqua green in Row 4 may be substituted for either of these two greens or may be used with them for added variety. A complete color scheme composed entirely of these four colors, with old gold as the one and only dominant color, has exciting possibilities.

The blue and rose in Row 3 make an excellent pair of dominants when used with color combinations from this first row. When blue and rose are used as dominants, the two greens in Row 3 are suggested for small single leaves or small leaf sprays. Old gold could be utilized for accent.

Blue and bright green, also from Row 3, are another excellent pair of dominants. With them use bright yellow green for accent. Old gold would not be included in this color scheme.

Row 2: Olive green*, golden brown, gold, khaki

These are more subdued colors than those found in the top row. They are all harmonious, and any two, any three, or all four of them may be used together in a pattern. They are particularly appropriate for leaves as well as stems, branches and trunks. When so used the accent color would be gold. All these colors may be used in approximately equal quantities, except for gold, which is used chiefly for contrast or accent.

Rust or brick (Row 4), or either of these paired with aqua blue (Row 4) make especially good

* Note: These first two rows contain the foundation colors of traditional crewel embroidery in the sense that so much of it is created around arboreal motifs—trees, branches, stems, leaves. The colors in Row 1, or in Row 2, can be used by themselves to create quietly interesting effects in small or medium-sized patterns. Muted, subdued tones are not quite so effective in large patterns and usually need the relief of some brighter colors.

dominant color choices. Rose and blue (Row 3) are also effective as dominants.

Aqua blue (Row 4) and gold (Row 2) make interesting dominant partners. Bring in green from Row 1 to team up with olive green on leaves. A good accent color is bright yellow green.

Row 3: Bright yellow green, rose, blue, bright green

These colors are also harmonious and may be used in any combinations of two, three or four. They should not be used in equal quantities, however, especially the two bright greens, which are best suited to accent roles. These two greens, *preferably in small quantities*, can be used as contrasts or accents in any color scheme. Rose and blue are contrasting colors and may be mingled with color combinations from either of the first two rows. All these colors, especially rose, can be effectively used to "lift" patterns with large quantities of the foundation colors from the first two rows. If you prefer, aqua blue (Row 4) or old blue (Row 5) may be substituted for this blue.

Row 4: Brick, aqua green, rust, aqua blue

These colors are all harmonious and any two, any three or all four of them may be used together in a pattern. They may be used in approximately equal quantities. Aqua green may be mingled with the greens of the first two rows to provide interesting variations. Rust and brick are excellent color companions when large quantities of the red family are to be used in a pattern. The blue in Row 3 may be substituted for aqua blue if desired.

Row 5: Purple, old blue, strawberry, grey (three values)

This is the "miscellaneous" row. Grey is used chiefly for animals. Strawberry is a fairly bright color, excellent as an accent when used in small quantities. Old blue blends well with greens for leaves and flowers; it lends subdued contrast, which can be very effective. Purple, generally used in modest quantities, blends well with almost any color combination on this chart.

The "triangle rule" as applied to the design used on the jacket and also shown in color following page 132.

The Triangle Rule

Color balance can also be achieved by means of symmetrical "islands" of color. For a simple experiment, glance once again at a map of the United States, as suggested earlier (refer to page 57). An effective way to handle a dominant color such as brilliant red would be to disperse moderately large areas of it in various places on the map. If it were used to color the state of Virginia, then a nice balance would be created by adding an area in the Far West, such as the state of Oregon. This now strikes an acceptable east-west balance, but it leaves the color somewhat concentrated in the upper portion of the map. Bringing Texas into the picture would balance this off nicely and would show a basically triangular distribution.

Observe the triangle rule as it applies to the jacket design following page 132. The pattern of this design, with three triangles superimposed upon it, is shown above. The triangle points lie in areas where balancing concentrations of colors are located.

The triangles and the colors they identify are:

> Rose, the primary dominant color
> Blue, the secondary dominant color
> Purple, the third dominant color

You will see at once that none of the three dominant colors may be described as outstandingly strong, vivid or challenging. Yet the whole design is, in fact, quietly colorful. These colors dominate partly because of their relative chromatic strengths

66

compared to the effect of the whole and partly because of the extent to which each is used.

Rose is used here as the primary dominant because it is a rich, warm color. Blue is not warm, but it is a good complement to rose and is used here in sufficient quantity to be of secondary importance. Purple, the third dominant, is a softly pleasant fusion of warm rose and cool blue and serves as an excellent "liaison" color. Gold, a warm, vibrant color, is actually a fourth dominant in this design. It was not "triangulated" on the pattern because three triangles seemed sufficient to illustrate the point.

As a general rule, three "islands" of any single dominant color are enough in any but really large pieces. Three triangles have been used in the sample design shown, but this does not mean that a piece must have three dominant colors. The most effective color schemes for some patterns employ only two dominant colors; in monochrome there is but one. Nor need the number of dominant colors be limited to three. The number of dominant colors used depends entirely upon the chromatic possibilities of the design.

Arranging your dominant colors around the points of imaginary triangles will aid toward achieving symmetrical balance across the design. You will not, of course, actually draw actual triangles on your design. Use your imagination and don't worry about attaining geometrical perfection. You will soon learn that you don't really need to handcuff yourself to this triangle rule; use it as a general guide to balanced color planning and let it go at that. In general, you will soon become aware that each dominant color should be used in more than one place, and in moderation, and that each significant color concentration is roughly equidistant from other concentrations of the same color.

You may or may not be able to place your dominant color choices in exact 1–2–3 sequences on the scale of importance. Don't let this worry you; in the final analysis your best judgment will give you what you really want, and that is the most important objective.

Dominant, Subordinate and Incidental Roles

The dominance of a bold color is often immediately apparent; it "hits you in the eye," so to speak. That is why strong colors should be used with restraint and why balanced distribution is so important. A concentration of bold color in just one area is like having a spotlight focused on that one place, overshadowing the rest of the design. When you divide and separate this concentration of color you diffuse the brilliance and bring the rest of the design into a more glowing light.

Generally speaking, the dominant role of a subordinate, more subdued color is not as immediately apparent unless it is used in really large quantities. Although they do not generate "spotlight" effects, soft colors too must be used in balance. Good color planning requires that dominant colors, whether bold or subdued, must be used in balanced distribution.

A further contribution to color diffusion is the incidental use of dominant colors. A close examination of the design following page 132 will show that use of the dominant colors is not restricted to areas immediately adjacent to the triangle points. Rose is the most obvious example. The *incidental* use of rose in small quantities here and there over the pattern is desirable; it is too warmly appealing to be used in only three concentrated areas. The incidental use of dominant colors in this manner gives stimulating accent to muted tones and can be employed most effectively. In the case of the abundant use of green, which is not classified here as one of the three selected dominant colors, please refer again, if necessary, to the discussion of the role of green in crewel embroidery (page 62).

The balancing of dominant colors has been especially emphasized because they are the most obvious colors, the ones most likely to "wreck" a piece if not handled well. However, all colors should be used in balanced distribution whether dominant, subordinate, contrast or accent. Subordinate, contrast and accent colors are normally used in smaller quantities than dominant colors and may be balanced somewhat more casually or ir-regularly—that is, a little to the right against a little to the left, a little at the top against a little at the bottom, etc.

Two additional observations on effective color balancing are:

Avoid strong dominant colors in small-scale pieces. No piece should ever be overwhelmed by a color, and this is likely to happen when small designs and bold colors are mixed. On your small pieces use softer, subdued tones. They can be more beautifully colorful by the use of restraint.

When there is an exact center unit in a design—a flower or leaf, perhaps—select a very quiet color, or combination of quiet colors, for this spot. The flower, or leaf, being in the very center, will attract attention by reason of its position on the pattern. To draw double attention to it by highlighting it in a strong color will throw the rest of the design out of balance and destroy the effect of the piece as a whole. Balance the center unit by touches of the same color, or colors, here and there around the outer edges of the pattern.

These general observations on the use of color in crewel embroidery reflect the experience of those who have worked with color over many years. Do accept them in the spirit of good friends standing steadfastly by to lend a hand—but don't let them spoil your fun.

Now, if you have completed Design I in mono-chrome, you are ready for your first venture into polychrome: Design II (page 69).

A RESUMÉ OF KEY POINTS IN COLOR PLANNING

Crewel colors are bright, gay, enchanting in their soft, flowing loveliness, occasionally bold but never harsh, garish or gauche.

Learn first to draw out the soft, muted qualities of color. Learn to blend adroitly, then seek bolder, headier, more challenging combinations.

Balance, balance, balance. Remember the #1 rule: Never use any color in just one place. Remember to use dominant colors also in incidental roles and blend in contrasting and accent colors with restraint.

Whenever you feel a tug of indecision in choos-ing between a vigorous and tranquil colors, go with the latter; when the bright and bold are wholly appropriate there will be no such inde-cision.

A box of freshly-sharpened colored pencils or crayons and a spare tracing of your design will prove invaluable aids in working out satisfying color schemes.

Stitch variations will also provide fascinating by-paths into the realm of color subtleties. Add as many as you can to your repertoire and learn how to use them effectively.

The most important key is you—with an occa-sional "assist" from those who have embroidered before you. Your pleasure and pride in creative artistry, in superb craftsmanship, are the ultimate goals.

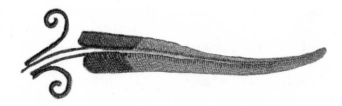

Courtesy Sir Isaac Pitman & Sons Ltd., London, England.
Embroidery and Needlework, *Gladys Windsor Fry.*

Design II (simple version), as used for a decoration on a handbag.

DESIGN II AND VARIATION

This design makes a beautiful decoration for a bag, as shown below, or it may be used effectively as a small pillow, a framed picture or tea cozy.

When either design has been completed you will be ready to attempt a more complex pattern (Design III, page 202). There you will find a larger canvas for your developing skills in stitching and color planning.

Working this design or its variation will add three more stitches to your repertoire: couching, French knots and long and short. Of these stitches, the long and short is the most important. It is used with great frequency in crewel embroidery and is featured here. Before starting this design this stitch should be mastered. Detailed instructions will be found on pages 102–104. Note particularly the importance of keeping long and short stitches in orderly alignment.

In this design you will be working with two colors. The finished piece shown in the photograph was worked in five values of aqua green, with two values of gold as an accent. Other combinations that go well together are: green and chocolate brown, rose and green, rust and aqua green, aqua blue and brick, blue and gold. In these pairings either color may be the dominant one, with the other used as an accent.

The design and its variation are shown below. The following two pages contain detailed drawings and notes covering all stitches and value sequences suggested for the individual units. In copying either pattern from the book onto your background material, please follow suggestions on page 53.

Before the piece is ready for use it must be finished and blocked. Complete directions are on pages 216–217.

1. Leaves in long and short, following value sequences and stitch directions, as shown on drawing. Tendrils worked in knot stitches.

2. Long and short stitches with value sequences just the reverse of those used in Drawing 1.

3. A. Couch in values #3 and #4, tied with value #5. French knots in each square worked in value #4 of a contrasting color.
   B. Solid chain stitches. Start with value #1 at outside edge and work to value #5 adjoining the couching.
   C. Long and short with value sequences as shown.
   D. Long and short, with value sequences as shown.

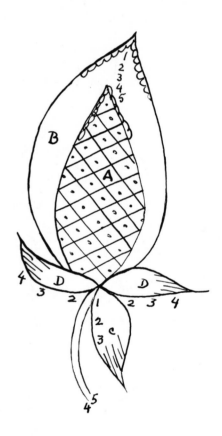

4. A. Satin stitch, value #1.
   B. Buttonhole stitch, value #3.
   C. Cretan stitch, value #4.
   D. Scattered seed stitches, value #3 of a contrasting color.
   E. Scattered French knots, value #4 of a contrasting color.

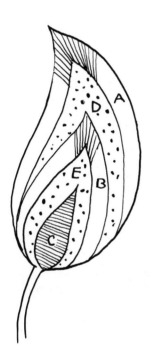

5. A. Solid long and short, with five values in sequence.
   B. Scalloped edge in outline stitch, value #1.
   C. Loop, in #3 of a contrasting color.

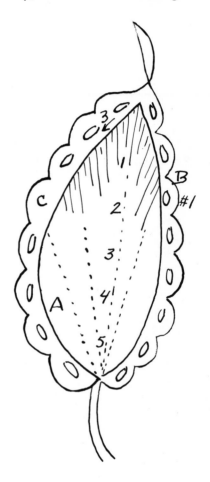

6. Attached fly stitches, value # 3.

Note: All stems on units in Design II are done in three rows of closely worked outline stitches, with value #4 in the middle, values #3 and #5 on the outside.

73

![decorative flourish] STITCHES

SOME 300 related stitches have been developed and perfected through the years in the process of creating fine embroidery. Perhaps one-third of these are used in crewel work. This book will cover approximately that range of stitches, providing an assortment varied enough to yield delightful results.

Primarily, the whole family of stitches springs from a group of four basic stitches:

1] The back stitch
2] The coral (or knot) stitch
3] The loop stitch
4] The running stitch

All embroidery stitches can be grouped in related categories as variations or combinations of these four basic stitches.

On the following pages about 100 stitches have been photographed. They are arranged in sequences headed by the basic stitches from which they originated. You may already be familiar with many of them.

A PICTORIAL SAMPLER

THE FOUR BASIC STITCHES

Back Stitch

Coral (Knot) Stitch

Loop Stitch

Running Stitch

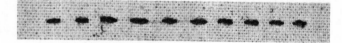

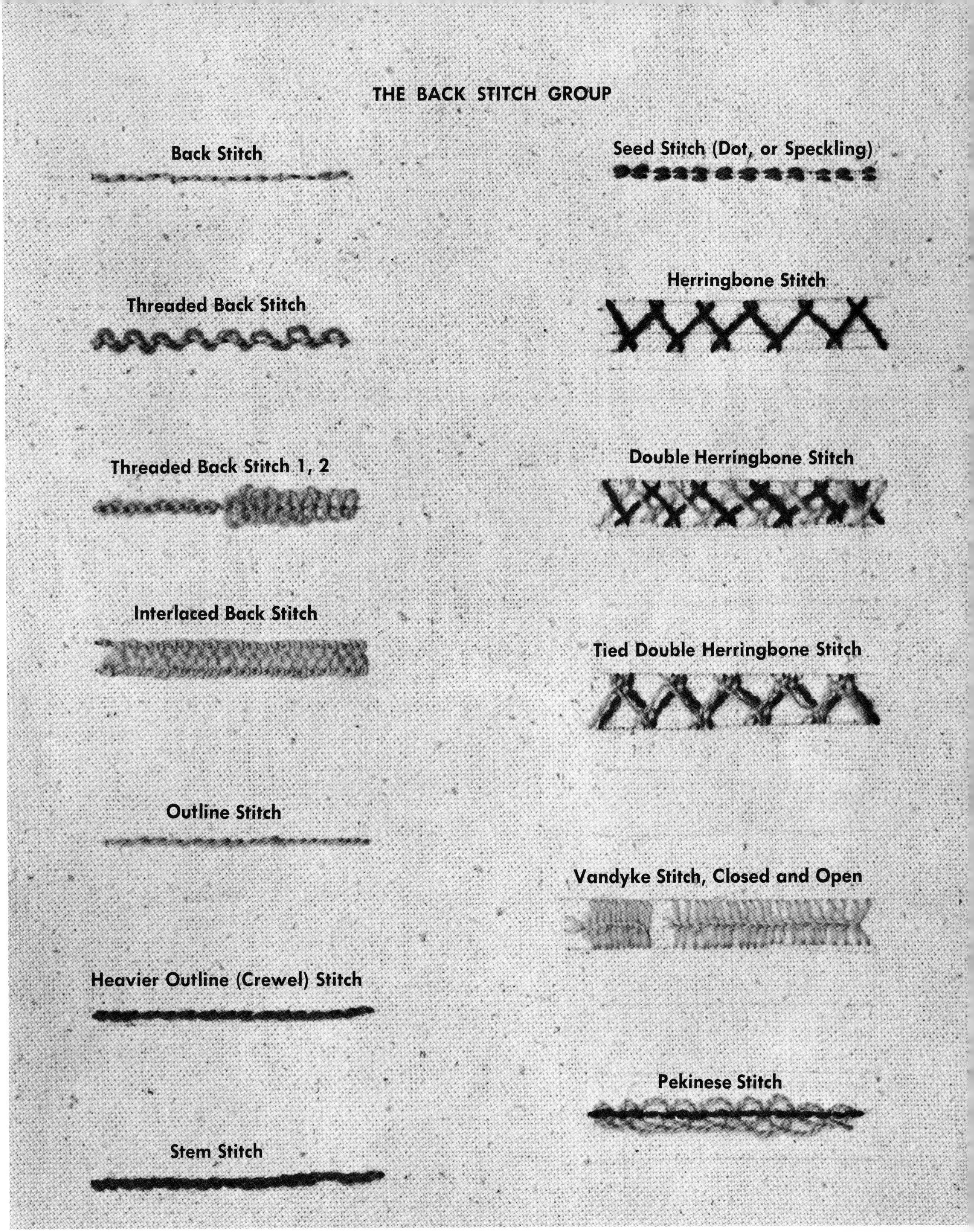

THE BACK STITCH GROUP

Back Stitch

Seed Stitch (Dot, or Speckling)

Threaded Back Stitch

Herringbone Stitch

Threaded Back Stitch 1, 2

Double Herringbone Stitch

Interlaced Back Stitch

Tied Double Herringbone Stitch

Outline Stitch

Vandyke Stitch, Closed and Open

Heavier Outline (Crewel) Stitch

Pekinese Stitch

Stem Stitch

Chevron Stitch

Threaded Herringbone Stitch

Raised Rose Stitch

Spider Web, Whipped and Woven

Closed Herringbone Stitch

Rumanian Stitch

Tied Threaded Herringbone Stitch

Whipped Stem Stitch

76

Coral (Knot) Stitch

Feather Stitch

Buttonhole Stitch

Closed Feather Stitch

Closed Buttonhole Stitch

Single Feather Stitch

Crossed Buttonhole Stitch

Long-Armed Feather Stitch

Open Buttonhole (Blanket) Stitch

Fish (Cretan) Stitch

Plaited Buttonhole Stitch

Whipped Buttonhole Stitch

77

Attached Buttonhole Stitch

Bullion Stitch

French Knot Stitch

Double Buttonhole Stitch

Cretan (Fish), Closed and Open

Open Fish (Cretan) Stitch, Woven

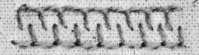

Cretan (Fish) Stitch, Tied

Buttonhole Stitch, Picot Edge

THE LOOP STITCH GROUP

Loop (Detached Chain) Stitch

Broad Chain Stitch

Chain Stitch

Heavy Chain Stitch

Wavy (Zig Zag) Chain Stitch

Tete de Boeuf Stitch

Open Chain Stitch

Attached Wheat Ear Stitch

Double Chain Stitch

Wheat Ear Stitch

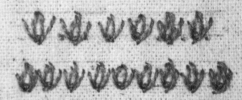

Twisted Chain Stitch

Whipped Chain Stitch

Checkered (Magic) Chain Stitch

Detached Fly Stitch

Threaded Chain Stitch 1

Attached Fly Stitch

Threaded Chain Stitch 2

Whipped Fly Stitch

Threaded Chain Stitch 3

Lazy Daisy Stitch

Russian Chain Stitch

Crested Chain Stitch

Double Chain Stitch, Crested

Senegalese Chain Stitch

Back-Stitched Chain Stitch

Straight Running Stitch

Basket Stitch

Whipped Running Stitch

Arrowhead Stitch

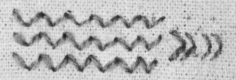

Interlaced Running Stitch

Zig Zag Stitch

Satin Stitch

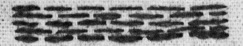

Sheaf Stitch

Darning Stitch

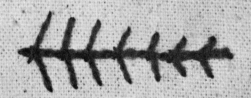

Cross Stitch

Thorn Stitch

Raised Band Stitch

SHADING STITCHES

Long and Short Stitch

Attached Buttonhole Stitch,

Closed and Open

Brick Stitch

Satin Stitch, Encroaching

Wave Stitch

Knot (Coral) Stitch

Stem (Outline) Stitch

Chain Stitch

FILLING STITCHES

Cross Stitch

Sword Stitch

Ermine Stitch

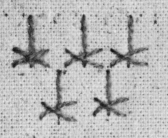

Four-Legged Knot Stitch

Sheaf (Fagot) Stitch

Star Stitch

Chessboard Stitch

Brick and Cross Stitch

83

Fly Stitch

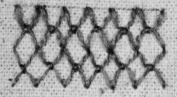

Cloud (Mexican) Stitch

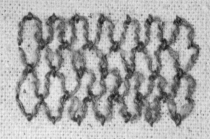

Honeycomb Filling

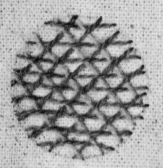

COUCHING (FILLING) STITCHES

Trellis 1

Trellis 2
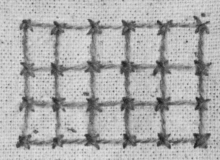

Trellis 3
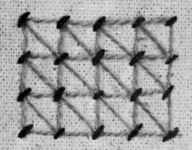

Trellis 4

Woven Couching

Battlemented Couching

Satin Stitch with Fly Stitch

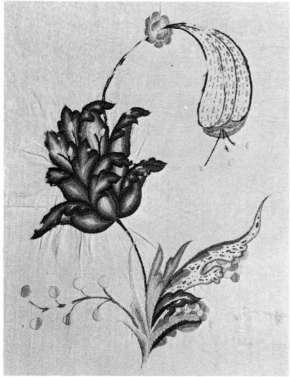

Of the 100-odd stitches in the Pictorial Sampler, about 60 have been selected for diagrammatic illustration accompanied by explanatory notes. These are the stitches most frequently encountered in crewel embroidery. If you wish to pursue stitch craftsmanship beyond this point, you may consult a number of excellent books, some of which are listed on page 218.

Here, two types of simple diagrammatic illustration have been used: (1) a stitch-tracking diagram indicating the path taken by the yarn in creating the stitch, and (2) a compact drawing of the completed stitch, or several completed stitches lying side-by-side. Some stitches are illustrated with both the diagram and the compact drawing, some with only the latter.

The tracking diagram is quite simple, usually consisting of straight lines plus a series of numbers starting with 1. In these diagrams you will see that you should start with the needle coming *out* through the material at 1, then going back *into* the material at 2, coming out again at 3, etc. In short, start at 1 and follow along in numerical sequence, with the needle coming *out* with the *odd* numbers (1-3-5, etc.) and going back *in* with the *even* numbers (2-4-6, etc.) For a demonstration of how the tracking diagram operates, turn to the first stitch diagram (page 88).

Tracking diagrams have been spread wide open in order to make it easy for you to follow the action. The finished stitches will, of course, be more like those pictured in the compact drawings. Do not follow the tracking diagram literally and spread your practice stitches wide-open; work them fairly close, so that they will consistently bear a close resemblance to the finished product, as shown.

Two motifs from a wide curtain believed to have been worked by a member or members of the Wade family of Ipswich, Mass., probably between 1725 and 1750. Another detail from this curtain is shown on page 49 and a part of the border is shown on page 162. *Courtesy Museum of Fine Arts, Boston, Mass.*

A working knowledge of from 80 to 100 stitches is not unusual, but many crewel embroiderers settle down to 40 or so favorite stitches as a basic working group. Better a master of 40 solidly useful stitches than a dabbler in twice as many, with indifferent results.

Diagrams of stitches, with accompanying instructions, are presented in this sequence.

1] The back stitch group.
2] The coral (or knot) stitch group.
3] The loop stitch group.
4] The running stitch group.
5] Long and short stitches. } shading stitches
6] Attached buttonhole stitch. }
7] Filling stitches.
8] Couching.
9] Laid work.

In the first four basic groups the "parent" stitch is discussed first and related stitches are given in the approximate order of their evolution from the parent stitches. Thus the "flow" from one stitch into another can be observed.

Long and short stitches are one of the most commonly used combinations in crewelwork, especially in shading. They are not particularly complex in themselves, but their application in some instances may become rather involved. Hence they are given detailed attention.

Attached buttonhole stitches are used primarily to achieve a shaded effect and are thus treated separately.

Filling stitches are many and varied, but they all perform the basic function implicit in their group name: that is, to fill otherwise-vacant spaces. They are among the most picturesque stitch patterns in all crewel embroidery.

Couching is an especially interesting form of space-filling. The variety of pleasing patterns and opportunities for handling color help to create focal points of interest. Detailed attention is also given to it.

Laid work is not actually a "stitch" at all, but its purpose is parallel to that of all filling stitches; therefore it is appropriately included here.

The first two designs in this book (Design I and Design II) incorporate 16 different stitches. Before completing the third design (Design III) you will add several others. This will get you off to a flying start. Thereafter you will add still others from time to time as the need arises, and almost before you know it you will have an impressive array of stitches at your fingertips.

Remember that your best needlework will be done with yarns not over two feet long. Longer yarns tangle easier, tend to become thin and drawn with repeated pulling and become quite soiled from handling.

Maintenance of continuity in stitch direction sounds simple enough, yet in twisting and turning for better light, a more comfortable working position, etc., a proper sense of orientation to the piece as a whole may very well be lost. In this situation take a pencil and lightly mark the correct stitch-paths on the material. The pencil-marks will be covered later by the embroidery.

Good crewel embroidery is anchored to the twill or other background material without knots. When starting a strand of yarn, bring it into the design with two or three back stitches. It will then be concealed by the embroidery. In the case of tendrils or other finely drawn lines it may seem difficult to anchor the yarn. In such cases approach the fine lines carefully by making almost invisible running stitches and finally a tiny back stitch. This will secure the yarn quite well, and of course the embroidery will be worked over it. When finishing a strand of yarn, turn the work on the wrong side and carefully weave the needle back and forth through the finished work so it does not show through the front. The work of an accomplished embroiderer is neat on both sides.

THE BACK STITCH GROUP

Back Stitch

Follow the tracking diagram: Out at 1, in at 2, out at 3, in at 4, etc., for as many stitches as necessary. Be sure the stitch lengths are uniform.

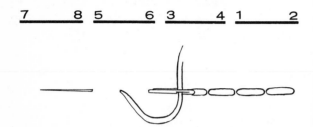

Threaded Back Stitch

First, make a row of even back stitches. Then, with a tapestry needle, weave yarn of a contrasting color back and forth, as illustrated by needle #1. For a heavier effect, weave in another value of the contrasting color in the manner shown by needle #2.

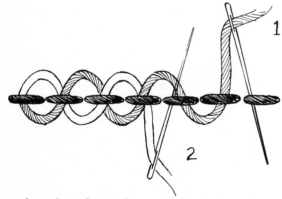

Interlaced Back Stitch

Make two rows of staggered back stitches arranged so that the ends of the stitches do not lie directly under each other. With a tapestry needle interlace yarn of a contrasting color from top to bottom, as shown in the diagram at the top of the next column.

Note: Refer to page 86 for details covering the two types of drawings used in this stitch section.

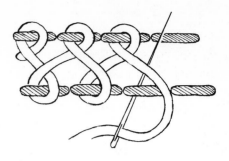

Outline Stitch

The important point here is to work with the yarn on the same side of the needle at all times. To the right or to the left as it may suit you, but keep it on the side you start. Oherwise a ragged appearance will ensue. To begin, bring the yarn up, and with the needle at a slight slant (either to the right or the left) pick up a bit of the material. Pull the yarn through and continue forward in this manner.

Stem Stitch

This is a heavier version of the outline stitch. Keep the yarn on the same side of a slanted needle, and pick up more material than with an outline stitch. The finished appearance is similar to that of closely worked small satin stitches.

Seed Stitches (Dot, Speckling)

These are tiny back stitches scattered irregularly over the surface to be covered.

Herringbone Stitch

Follow the tracking diagram: Out at 1, in at 2, out at 3, in at 4, out at 5, etc. This stitch may be tied at the intersections, using a contrasting color for best effects.

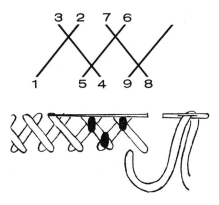

Double Herringbone Stitch

Make two rows of interlocking stitches, using two contrasting colors or two values of the same color. Complete one row first, then work the other into it, as illustrated.

Tied Threaded Herringbone Stitch

After completing the herringbone stitches form a knot over each intersection, using a contrasting color or another value of the same color.

Chevron Stitch

Follow the tracking diagram: Out at 1, back in at 2, out again at 3, etc., following the sequence shown. Where the lines come together in a point the yarn first goes in, then later comes out through that exact spot. Going in, it is called 4; coming out, it is called 7. The same is true of 8 and 11 and also 12 and 15.

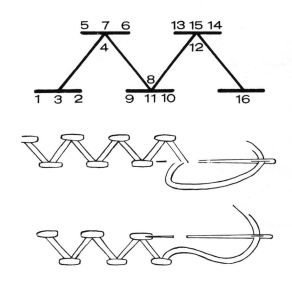

Rumanian Stitch

Long closely worked back stitches tied in the center with very small back stitches. The material should not show through.

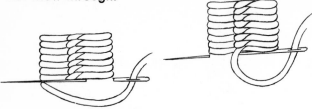

Bokhara (Couching)*

In essence these are Rumanian stitches tied several times at irregular intervals instead of being tied just once at the center.

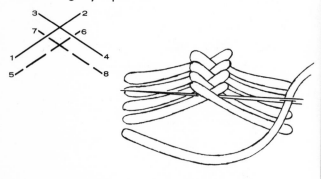

Vandyke Stitch

Follow the tracking diagram: Out at 1, back in at 2, out again at 3, etc., following the sequence shown. The 5-6 and 7-8 yarns go under the 1-2 and 3-4 yarns. In like manner all succeeding yarns are worked under those laid just before—without picking up the material. The other diagram shows stitches slightly opened.

* Note: For couching stitches see page 108.

Spider Web

Start here laying yarns across an imaginary circle. After the yarns (spokes) are laid you will need a tapestry needle for the spiral portion of the web. A tapestry needle may be used for spoke-laying too. You may lay three, four or five yarn strands for the spokes. Here four have been laid. When the spokes have been completed, tie them all together at the center, but do not tie them to the material.

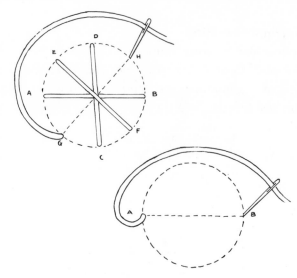

Here a tapestry needle is used. Bring the yarn up at the center and slide it under spokes A and E. Next, loop it around E and carry it under D; then loop it around D and carry it under H, etc. In the diagram the needle is forming the loop around F and is sliding under C.

For a tightly filled effect, work the spirals in close together. The ridges should be even and should stand out. Many prefer a looser effect with visible spokes to heighten the image of a spider's web.

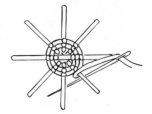

90

THE CORAL (KNOT) STITCH GROUP

Coral (Knot) Stitch

Bring the yarn up through the material and drape it in a loop. Then slide the needle under the right side of the loop, through a small portion of the material and over the left side of the loop. Pull the needle through and a small knot will be formed. Repeat, keeping the knots fairly close together.

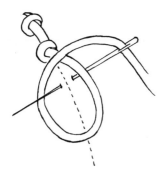

Buttonhole Stitch

Before starting, mark the path these stitches are to follow by making parallel rows of small running stitches (the broken lines in the drawing). This gives the work a slightly raised and more finished appearance.

Start as in the tracking diagram: Out at 1, in at 2, out at 3 (just a fraction to the left of 1), then in at 4, out at 5, bringing the needle over the bottom of the loop. Continue with the loop-4-5 action. The material should not show through the stitches.

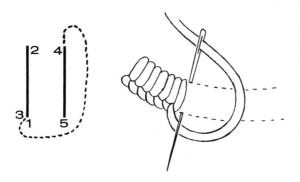

Open Buttonhole (Blanket) Stitch

Proceed as with plain buttonhole, except that the stitches are spaced well apart, as shown in drawing.

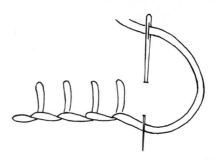

Closed Buttonhole Stitch

Similar to the open buttonhole, with the stitches slanted together at the top, as illustrated.

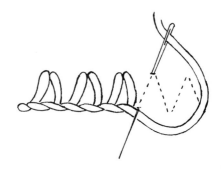

Crossed Buttonhole Stitch

Similar to the closed buttonhole stitch, with the stitches slanted so they cross, as in the drawing.

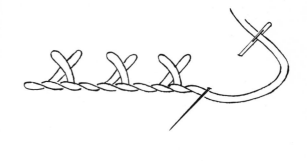

Double Buttonhole Stitch

Mesh two rows of open buttonhole stitches, as illustrated.

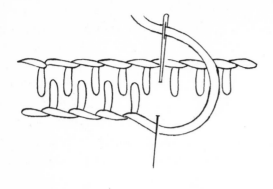

Feather Stitch

Start by coming out at 1, then loop the yarn to 2 (holding it with thumb), in at 2, out at 3 over the loop, then make another loop, in at 4, and continue in this manner. Note how the loops alternate—first to the right, then to the left.

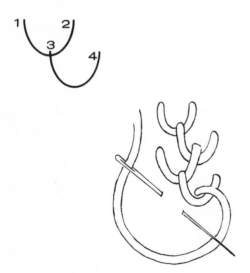

Cretan (Fish) Stitch, Open

The action is similar to that of the feather stitch, with shallow loops. Follow the tracking diagram, starting out at 1, in at 2, out at 3 over the 1-2 yarn, in at 4, to complete the first step. Repeat with 5 coming out just to the left of, and then over, the 3-4 yarn. Note how the stitches broaden toward the base.

Cretan (Fish) Stitch, Closed

Same as the open Cretan, with the stitches worked closely so the material does not show through.

French Knot

Bring the yarn up through the material, form a loop, put the needle back into the material just to the right of the point where it came out. Leave the needle inserted in the material and pull the loop firmly around the needle shaft. Hold the yarn in position with the thumb while the needle is pulled through to form a perfect knot.

Bullion Knot

Sometimes called a French knot, the bullion knot serves the same purpose although it is larger, heavier and stands higher. Bring the yarn up through the material and wind it around the needle a couple of times. Put the needle back into the material just to the right of the point where it came out. Hold the twisted yarn with your thumb while the needle is gently pulled all the way through to form a knot.

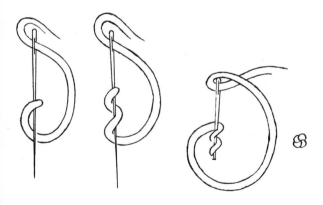

Bullion Stitch

Start by bringing the yarn up through the material at A. Then re-insert the needle at B and bring it out as close to A as you can, but do not pull it completely through. Now, take six or seven turns of the yarn around the needle (more if you wish). Hold the coiled yarn with the thumb while the needle is pulled completely through. As you pull the strand taut the coil will turn up end-over-end so the completed stitch will lie between A and B. Anchor the B end, and continue with other coils until the space is filled with coiled yarns placed neatly side by side.

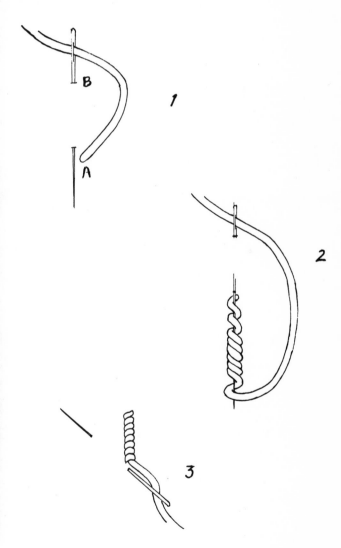

93

THE LOOP STITCH GROUP

Loop (Detached Chain) Stitch

Bring the yarn up at A, form a closed U-shaped loop and reinsert the needle close to A as shown, bringing it out over the loop bottom. Next, insert the needle just under the loop and pull the yarn through, thus anchoring the loop.

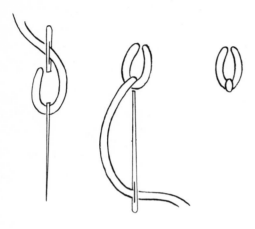

Lazy Daisy Stitch

When loop stitches are arranged in a circular pattern the resultant figure is called a lazy daisy.

For a double lazy daisy, first make a small loop stitch, then fit a larger one snugly around it, as in the small drawing.

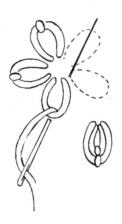

Detached Fly Stitch

The action is identical with that of the regular loop stitch except that the completed stitch is V-shaped. It is tied in the same manner. Normally, these stitches are made fairly close together.

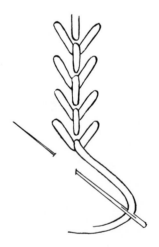

Attached Fly Stitch

Very similar to the detached fly stitch except that the anchoring stitch is elongated in order to create the impression that the stitches are all tied together.

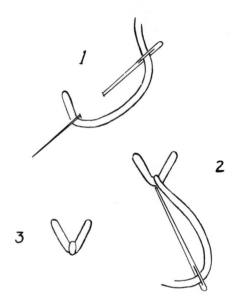

Whipped Fly Stitch

With a tapestry needle whip a length of attached fly stitches with a yarn of a contrasting color, being careful not to pick up the material in the process.

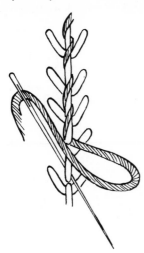

Wheat Ear Stitch

This is a combination of regular loop and detached fly stitches. Be sure the fly stitch is spread so its wings stand out from the loop. In some stitch books this Wheat Ear Stitch is called the Tete de Boeuf.

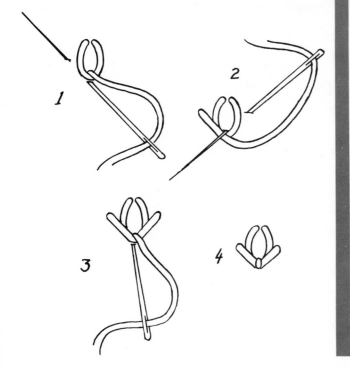

Tete de Boeuf Stitch

First, work two straight running stitches at an angle to each other—suggesting a wide V (not joined at the bottom). Then, as in the drawing, work a loop stitch over the running stitches. Tie the bottom of the loop, as shown.

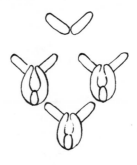

Attached Wheat Ear Stitch

Attachment is accomplished by working each new loop behind the fly stitch just above it.
The longer chain is a modified form of attached wheat ears—almost but not quite touching.

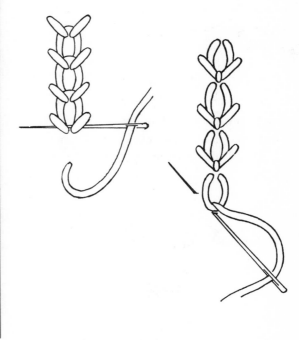

95

Chain Stitch

This is a progression of loop stitches. The manner by which the loops are linked is clearly shown in the drawing. Be careful to keep the loop sizes uniform.

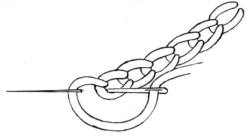

Twisted Chain Stitch

Start as with an ordinary loop stitch, but in coming back for completion of the loop swing to the left so that the yarns cross at the top. Start the next twisted chain by bringing the needle out and over the bottom of the loop just made.

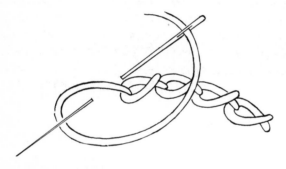

Wavy (Zig Zag) Chain Stitch

Similar to the chain stitch, with loops alternately slanting to the right and to the left. To hold the loops flat, complete each new loop by running the needle through the yarn at the bottom of the loop just above.

Open Chain Stitch

Almost identical with the normal chain stitch, except that the loop tops are much more open. The manner by which the loops are linked is clearly shown in the drawing. Be careful to keep the loop sizes uniform.

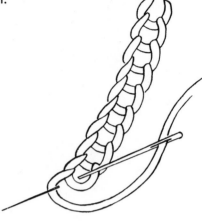

Double Chain Stitch

Start by forming an open chain loop from 1 to 2 (the bottom loop). Then, bring the needle out at 3 over the first loop and form another loop from 3 back to 1. Next, form another loop in similar manner from 3 to 4. Continue in this fashion, alternating the loops from right to left. Start each new loop by bringing the yarn from the inside, and over, the previous loop. Be careful to keep the loop sizes uniform.

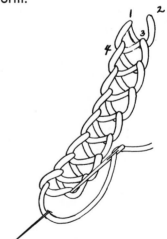

Checkered (Magic) Chain Stitch

This is a normal chain stitch worked with two yarn strands instead of one. Thread two different-colored yarns into the needle. Then, start a normal chain stitch, keeping one yarn strand under the needle, the other over the needle. With the next loop reverse the over-and-under position of the yarns. Only the yarn worked under the needle will form a loop; hence this procedure will form a series of loops in alternating colors, each loop tied into the other as with an ordinary chain.

Broad Chain Stitch

Start at 1 with a small vertical running stitch. Then, make an "upside-down" loop, running the yarn under the vertical stitch without picking up the material. Continue with successive loops, running each loop under the one before without picking up the material.

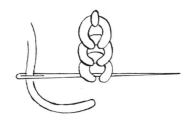

Heavy Chain Stitch

Start at 1 with a small vertical running stitch. Then, make an "upside-down" closed loop. The first loop is carried under the vertical stitch without picking up the material. Continue with successive loops, running each loop behind the second one above it without picking up the material.

Threaded Chain Stitch

Make a row of detached chain stitches, as shown. Then, with a tapestry needle, weave yarns of a contrasting color (or two contrasting colors if you wish) through the loops without picking up the material.

Whipped Chain Stitch

Use a tapestry needle to whip yarn of a contrasting color diagonally around a row of attached chain stitches without picking up the material.

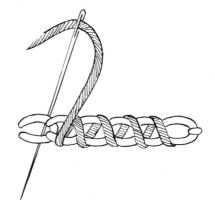

Back-Stitched Chain Stitch

Use yarn of a contrasting color to run a series of small back stitches through a chain row, placing them over the point where the loops adjoin each other.

Crested Chain Stitch

A] Start by making a small loop at point 1 on the top drawing, then bring the yarn back up through this loop.

B] At point 2 drape the yarn in a loop and then weave the needle in and out of the material so it lies under and over the yarn as shown. Pull the needle through and form a knot, as in the second drawing.

C] Without catching up the material, go under the 1-2 yarn strand, as in the second drawing.

D] Insert the needle into the material through the small loop (third drawing) and bring it out a short distance below this loop, and over the yarn you are about to pull through. Pull the yarn through, and the first stitch will be completed.

From this point you can immediately go over to make the knot (at 3) for the second crested stitch, and then continue the action as with the first stitch.

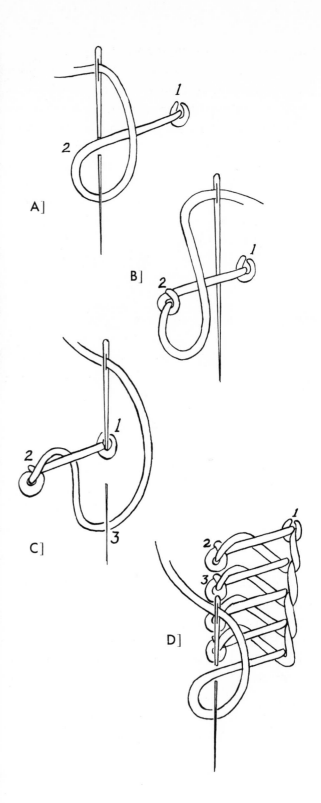

THE RUNNING STITCH GROUP

Straight Running Stitch

Working from right to left, the needle simply goes in and out of the material, creating a row of uniform stitches spaced at regular intervals.

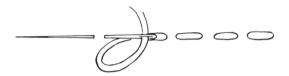

Whipped Running Stitch

Use a tapestry needle to overcast yarn of a contrasting color, as illustrated, without picking up the material.

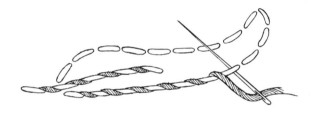

Interlaced Running Stitch

Make two rows of identical running stitches, each stitch lying directly under the one above. Then, use a tapestry needle to weave yarn of a contrasting color (or two contrasting colors if you wish) back and forth, as shown, without picking up the material.

Darning Stitch

These are small running stitches and should be made to lie in alternating rows, as shown. The stitch action is clearly shown by the needle. Many interesting needlework patterns can be created with this simple stitch.

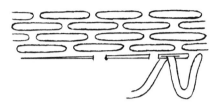

Arrowhead Stitch

These small V-shaped stitches (open at the bottom) may be arranged in many interesting patterns, as suggested by the diagrams. The stitching action is clearly demonstrated by the needle.

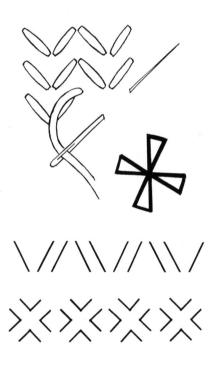

Cross Stitch

Follow the tracking diagram: Out at 1, in at 2, out at 3, in at 4, etc., to the end of the row. Then come back: in at 7, out at 8, etc., until all the crosses have been completed. The crosses may be connected or slightly separated, as desired.

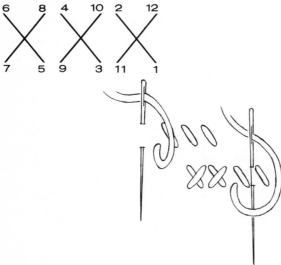

Satin Stitch

This is simply a running stitch worked closely so that the material does not show through. There are two important points to remember in using this stitch: (1) First, outline the working area with small back stitches (the broken line shown on the drawing). This helps to give the completed work a finished appearance. (2) Keep the stitch directions uniform; otherwise the work will appear uneven and disorderly. If you have difficulty with stitch direction, mark stitch paths on the material before you start. Variety may be attained by dividing a unit (a leaf, for example) and arranging the stitches in each half so they slant toward the center vein.

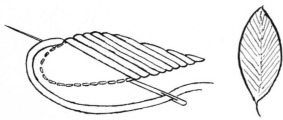

Thorn Stitch

First, lay a vertical yarn strand from A to B, anchoring it at the A end. Carry the yarn through the material at B, but leave a short length of it hanging loose so that you can work around curves, such as tendrils, if necessary. Then, follow the tracking diagram: Out at 1, in at 2, out at 3, in at 4, etc. The thorns become longer as they are worked toward the bottom. Do not forget to anchor the yarn at B.

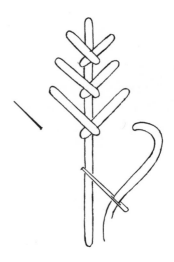

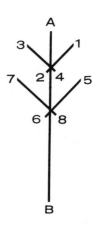

Simple Sheaf Stitch

A] Lay horizontal foundation yarns in pairs for the full length of the area to be covered, forming bars as at A-B-C-D.

B] Next, with a tapestry needle, lay vertical satin stitches over bars A and B, as shown. When this block has been completed, repeat the process between bars B and C, working the new stitches between those previously laid. Continue in this manner until all the blocks are filled. Do not pick up the material in this process.

C] Finally, the sheaf effect is created by placing two small horizontal stitches in the center of each block and pulling the other stitches gently together. Here the material is picked up to prevent the binder yarns slipping down out of position.

Heavy Raised Band Stem Stitch

First, lay closely worked vertical yarns side by side over the area to be covered. This foundation will give the finished work a built-up appearance.

Next, make a series of single-strand horizontal bars, as in the illustration.

Now, using a tapestry needle, start below the right end of the bottom bar and carry the yarn straight up and around the bar next above. Continue in this manner to the top, return to the bottom and repeat the process unil the band is completed. Do not pick up the material in this action.

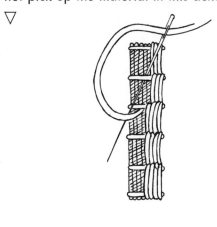

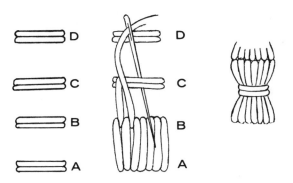

Simple Raised Band Stem Stitch

First, lay a series of single-strand horizontal bars similar to those in the sheaf stitch.

Now, using a tapestry needle, start below the right end of the bottom bar and carry the yarn straight up and around the bar next above. Continue in this manner to the top, then return to the bottom and repeat the process until the band is completed. Do not pick up the material in this action.

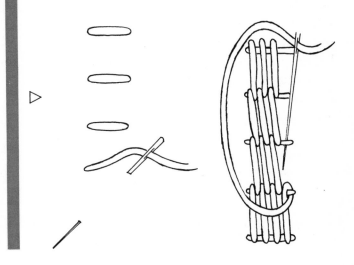

SHADING STITCHES:
LONG AND SHORT AND
ATTACHED BUTTONHOLE

This stitch combination is one of the most invaluable and most widely used in the whole scope of crewel embroidery. The following notes cover stitch techniques and blending of colors.

Long-and-short has been described in many extravagant terms, both admiringly and despairingly. One of the best descriptions is simple and to the point: "Staggered long and short satin stitches flowing symmetrically over a unit." The real secret of successful long and short work lies in the word "symmetrical." There is nothing very difficult about making a pair of simple long and short stitches. Problems, if any, arise in adapting them to the multitude of irregular contours that abound in crewel embroidery.

Three aids in keeping your stitches "flowing symmetrically" are:

1] Continuity of stitch direction. Once the directional path has been plotted, all stitches must flow in that direction. Plotting stitch paths on the material in light pencil lines is suggested—at least until you gain ease in working this stitch combination. How stitch paths are plotted for leaves and flower petals will be fully illustrated below.

2] Working stitch rows in alternating directions. When the first row of stitches is worked from left to right the next row is worked in the opposite direction—right to left. The third row is worked from left to right, as was the first row. Continue alternating the direction of each row.

3] Stitch action, the first-row stitches are made working the yarn from the top of the stitch to the bottom of the stitch. This action holds for the *first row only*. In succeeding rows the action is reversed: that is, the yarn is worked from the bottom of the stitch to the top of the stitch. Stitches in the second row, and all succeeding rows, are worked up into previously completed stitches.

Continuity is essential; the techniques discussed in paragraphs (2) and (3) are optional but

strongly recommended. Working rows in alternating directions and working stitches up into previously completed stitches will result in better control and a more satisfying appearance.

The tracking diagram below illustrates all three points. The stitch paths run in a straight line (up and down in this case); the first row (solid lines) is worked from left to right as the horizontal arrow indicates; the second row (dotted lines) is worked in the opposite direction; the third row (solid lines again) is worked from left to right; the stitches in the first row are worked from top to bottom and those in the second and third rows from bottom to top, as indicated by the vertical arrows.

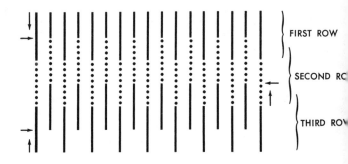

In this simplified tracking diagram the stitch paths happen to go straight up and down. You are not likely, however, to encounter such a neatly convenient arrangement very often. In any event, the same working principles apply whether the stitch paths are vertical, horizontal or diagonal.

This diagram also highlights the fact that normally only the first and last rows contain both long and short stitches. The in-between rows all contain long stitches. The third row, if it were the last row, would need a series of short stitches along the bottom to fill the unit completely. This is the normal stitch pattern, varied occasionally to meet special situations, such as when two or more short stitches in succession are required in working around a curve.

Three leaves in which directional paths have been plotted are illustrated as aids in planning long and short work in your own units. These leaves show three basic patterns of stitch direction: (1) diagonally across the leaf, (2) basically from top to bottom yet with slight diagonal action toward the stem, and (3) diagonally from each side directly to the center vein. Study your leaf to decide which flow pattern best suits your particular needs. Then mark the material lightly in pencil to indicate it before beginning to embroider.

LONG AND SHORT STITCHES

Leaf 1

Stitch paths are indicated by the broken diagonal lines. The first row of stitches will begin on the scalloped edge, and this has been marked on the material also.

Each successive row, of course, follows the stitch paths straight across the leaf.

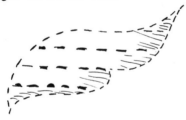

Leaf 2

Here the first row is placed at the top of the leaf, as marked on the drawing. Succeeding rows follow the stitch paths (broken lines) to the stem. As the leaf broadens toward the center the stitch rows must be made wider, then contracted again as the leaf narrows toward the base.

Leaf 3

This leaf is worked in two sections, from the outside edges to the center line. Complete one-half, then work the other half, keeping them as much alike as you can. Plot stitch directions and sketch in the two first rows (one for each half) on the material before you begin. After completing the long and short work, run an outline-stitch vein down the center line.

Long and short stitches are ideal for subtle color-blending. The best results are obtained from effective use of value sequences rather than a number of different colors. In general, use at least two values of any color introduced into a unit. However, a single value of a color is often used in "tipping" the edges of a leaf or petal, following which values are often used in sequences of two or more. Values should flow naturally and smoothly from one into another.

The number of colors, or color values, should be commensurate with the size of the unit. Do not crowd the design just to include a lot of color. Create the feeling of "flowing" color just as you seek to create a feeling of rhythm in the stitches.

Two diagrams of flower petals, with color and value-sequence notations, are given on the following page. These are but a sample of the many possible color combinations. These color suggestions may be accommodated to smaller petals by eliminating one or more values nearest the base.

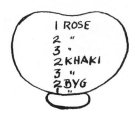

The contours of flower petals usually require more careful planning than do leaf outlines, especially when the stitch paths converge toward the base. A petal in three successive stages of long and short development is illustrated below.

Drawing 1

The directional paths (broken lines) have been plotted from the outside edge to the base of the petal, and the first row of stitches sketched in.

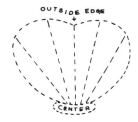

Drawing 2

The first row has been completed. It was worked from the center of the petal to one side, then from the center to the other side, as shown by the arrows. Working from the center to the sides allows better control over stitch action.

Here alternating directions are found in the first row. To alternate directions in succeeding rows, simply treat the petal as if the right half were one unit, the left half another unit, and alternate each half separately. This is detailed in Drawing 3.

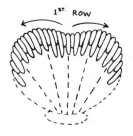

Drawing 3

Here the petal was turned so the second row could be worked into the first row; the third row into the second, etc. Note how snugly the stitches all fit into each other.

The second-row stitches were worked from the edges to the center (the white arrows) and the third-row stitches from the center to the edges, thus providing alternating row-directions.

ATTACHED BUTTONHOLE STITCH

Attached Buttonhole Stitch

This is called an attached buttonhole stitch because it is actually attached to the material. A detached buttonhole stitch is not attached to the material. Start at the outside of the unit and work one row of buttonhole stitches, spacing them ever so slightly apart. The second row is worked *into* the first row, and this process is continued until the unit is completely filled. For a lacy appearance keep the stitches spread slightly apart; for a solid surface work the stitches closely.

This stitch is especially adaptable to the creation of subtly pleasing shading effects, particularly in leaves and flower petals. This is accomplished by using a different value for each row, beginning with one of the darker values in the first row and using successively lighter values for each added row.

FILLING STITCHES

Filling stitches are those best suited to the creation of attractive stitch and color effects in spaces that would otherwise be empty. Stitches employed in filler roles also have other uses elsewhere.

In addition to stitches described here under the heading "Filling Stitches," there are many others that may be used effectively: Seed, French and Bullion Knots, Loops, Lazy Daisy, Fly, Tete de Boeuf, Wheat Ear, Running (Darning), Arrowhead, Cross—and any others that appeal to you. These are all described in their own category. Refer to the index for page locations.

Filling stitches present an excellent opportunity to bring in interesting accent and contrasting colors. Do not neglect these color possibilities. There are countless pattern arrangements for space-filling, A few of them are illustrated here. Designing your own arrangements is the most fun of all. Try it.

These are just a few of the wealth of interesting pattern arrangements available for space-filling. The emphasis here is on patterns rather than stitches. If, for example, you feel that sheaves would be more effective than the stitch figure suggested in the pattern you are copying, then by all means feel free to substitute sheaves.

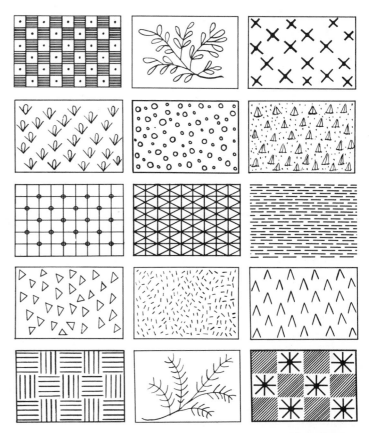

(*Bottom*) A sampler of satin filling stitches. *Courtesy Sir Isaac Pitman & Sons, Ltd., London.* Embroidery and Needlework, *Gladys Windsor Fry.*

FILLING STITCHES

Four-Legged Knot Stitch
This is an upright cross stitch with a knot made directly over the center where the stitches cross. The knot is made without picking up the material.

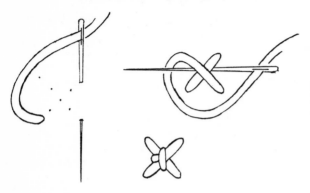

Ermine Stitch
One vertical yarn strand crossed diagonally by two shorter yarn strands.

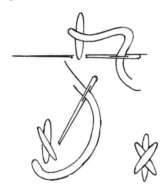

Star Stitch
The star begins with one vertical stitch. If the star is to have six points, add two diagonal crossing stitches. If it is to have eight points (as this one does) add a horizontal stitch also. The star may be tied in the center with a small stitch.

Sheaf (Fagot) Stitch
Lay three or four yarns side by side. Pull together in the middle with two small stitches to form a "bundle." A slight variation may be had by laying two stitches diagonally, as shown in the bottom drawing.

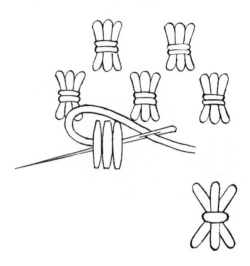

Cloud Stitch
First, lay several rows of small vertical back stitches in the alternating pattern shown on the drawing. Then, using a tapestry needle, and yarn of a contrasting color if you wish, work yarn strands through the back stitches, forming "clouds," as illustrated.

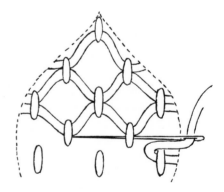

Fly Stitch

These stitches, attached or detached, may be arranged to form various interesting patterns.

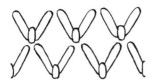

Brick and Cross Stitch

Make the bricks first, using the same number of horizontal satin stitches in each brick. Then, with yarn of a contrasting color, make the crosses, tying them in the center. Bricks and crosses alternate, as shown.

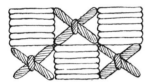

Chessboard Stitch

This stitch is used to build rows of satin-stitch blocks alternating with open spaces of the same size. Keep the same number of stitches in each block. Finish by working crosses in yarn of a contrasting color.

Honeycomb Filling

First, lay evenly spaced horizontal yarns, using a dark values.

Here, lay evenly spaced diagonal yarns, using a medium value.

Finally, using a tapestry needle, weave a lighter-value yarn in the other diagonal direction. Weave over and under, as illustrated.

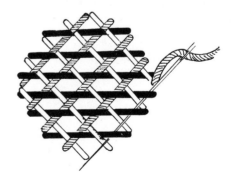

COUCHING STITCHES

Trellis 1
First, lay evenly spaced vertical yarns then over them lay evenly spaced horizontal yarns. Tie each intersection with yarn of a contrasting color.

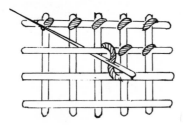

Trellis 2
Same as #1, except that it is tied with small crosses.

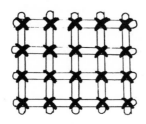

Trellis 3
To the Trellis #1 pattern add diagonal yarns. Tie, as shown.

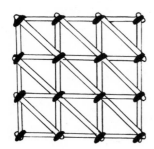

Trellis 4
First, lay two yarns as in #1, then work a covering cross in each square. Tie the crosses with small back stitches. For the final tie-down use cross stitches as shown.

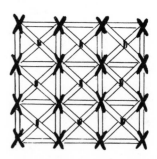

Battlemented Couching
Four sets of vertical and horizontal yarns are laid, one set on the other. Four color values are used, in this case from light on the bottom to dark on top (or, if you prefer, from dark on the bottom to light on top).

Lay the first set of yarns as in Trellis 1. The second set is laid to the left and below the first set. Continue in the same manner with sets three and four.

Each set of yarns will tie down the set under it. Refer to the drawing for tie-down of the fourth set.

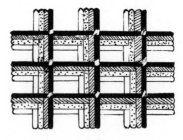

Note: Couching is most interesting when done with color variations. Use value sequences from dark on the bottom through medium in the middle (when there are diagonal yarns) to light on top; or in reverse order if you prefer. Tie in yarn of a contrasting color.

LAID WORK

Laid work is one of the easiest and quickest ways to fill stems, tree branches, leaves and similar spaces. It is essentially a series of yarn strands laid side by side and then tied to the background material by an overlay of couching, open chain stitches or fly stitches.

The two most popular methods for laid work differ chiefly in the way in which the yarn-ends are anchored to the material. These are shown at right. Select the method you prefer, but do try to keep your laid-work strands close together.

Normally, only one color value is used with laid work. A gradation of values can be used, of course, but the end result is not worth the extra effort. Sufficiently pleasing color effects can be achieved by using attractive contrasting colors for the tie-down.

Other examples of laid work are given in Design Units 7–12, 47–52 and 58. Observe in Unit 52 how beautifully laid work fits in with other stitch combinations.

A sampler of open filling stitches. *Courtesy Sir Isaac Pitman & Sons, Ltd., London.* Embroidery and Needlework, *Gladys Windsor Fry.*

1] In the first method *both ends* of the yarn strands are anchored to the material by tiny stitches taken at each end of the individual strands as they are laid. When all the strands are completely anchored the tie-down stitches are made. Under this system of first anchoring both ends the strands all lie in a straight line. This method is quite satisfactory for filling leaves and similar spaces but is difficult to use around a curve.

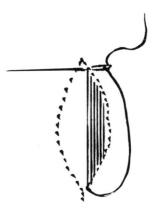

2] Under the alternate method the yarn strands are anchored at *one end only* until the tie-down has been almost completed. When all strands have been anchored at the starting end, straighten and smooth them and place them under your thumb. Now, proceed with tying, starting at the anchored end and working toward the loose end. Your thumb will guide the strands and hold them in position. Here, as you see, a curve may be handled quite effectively. When the tie-down is completed, anchor the loose ends by bringing them through the material and weaving them into the reverse side of the pattern. It is suggested that you do not work with more strands than you can comfortably hold under your thumb at one time.

CHAPTER FIVE

CREWEL EMBROIDERY
FOR INTERIOR DECORATION
AND PERSONAL USE

ALTHOUGH decorative crewel pieces for the home (fire screens, draperies, chair-coverings, wall panels, framed pictures and similar appointments) are currently featured in many popular homemakers' magazines, crewel motifs for personal adornment were greatly prized by both ladies and gentlemen in an earlier era. Waistcoats, gloves, purses, caps, scarves, slippers, bodices, petticoats and other apparel, including aprons and workbags, bore the imprint of loving handiwork. An exquisite wedding gown embroidered in flowers and winding tendrils by a New England bride of the 1730's has been preserved by the Wadsworth Atheneum of Hartford, Connecticut, which has a fine collection of crewel embroidery, both American and English.

The glass of fashion is not likely to return to those candlelit parlors, but crewel embroidery has inspired many attractive personal uses today. Crewel colors and stitches need not be confined to

Knitting or sewing bag. *Embroidered by Mrs. Arthur Lewis, Walpole, Mass.*

110

traditional shades and motifs, nor should it be considered solely a feminine province. Consider, for instance, the effectiveness of a solid-color tie decorated in a two-toned spray of pussy willows or leaves, a blazer or jacket with an emblem, a sweater, scarf or muffler, a crewel-embroidered vest or weskit for special masculine gatherings.

Women's apparel does, of course, lend itself to a broader application of the crewel art. Just a few possibilities are pictured in this section—a sweater, jacket, dress, belt and handbags. You might add to the list negligees, bedjackets, housecoats, hats, collars, cuffs, vests, lingerie, stocking, jewelry and eyeglass cases enhanced by fine needlework.

A few simple designs are given on the next pages. These are but a few of the almost limitless possibilities. If you want to try your hand at designing, here is an excellent place to begin. Start, for instance, by making a simple unit that can be repeated as a skirt border and go on from there.

The technique for transferring a design to a piece of wearing apparel is not quite the same as for a square of twill. For one thing, you would not want to trace a design directly upon a sweater or jacket. You would find that it is far more satisfactory to trace the design upon a piece of loosely woven organdy or similar material. Baste the organdy design onto the sweater, jacket or other garment just where you wish the decoration to appear and then work the embroidery through the organdy directly into the garment itself. The embroidery technique is the same as for working on twill, except that you do not use a hoop or frame, which might stretch the material or wool too much. You must be careful not to pull your strands of wool yarn so tight that the material will pucker. It does take patience and persistence, but the results will justify your efforts. When the embroidery has been completed, remove the basting stitches and then gently pull out the organdy threads. Here you may find a pair of tweezers a help.

These articles are finished and blocked in this way: Place the embroidered area face down on a fluffy turkish towel and press lightly with a steam iron until all wrinkles and stray puckers are gone.

A Connecticut bride—Mary Myers Johnson—is said to have embroidered her own wedding gown in crewel yarns in 1732. Olive green predominates, combined with shades of rose, golds and a little blue. *Photograph by E. Irving Blomstrann. Courtesy Wadsworth Atheneum, Hartford, Conn.*

DESIGN UNITS FOR
PERSONAL USE

Five designs (A–E) suitable for the decoration of wearing apparel or accessories are given below. All may be used alone or repeated on belts, skirt or petticoat borders, etc. A few smaller designs are also included below.

Unit A, as well as Units B and C, has been designed to be repeated as a row of separate motifs not directly touching each other. Units D and E may also be used in this fashion, but they are especially adaptable to use as connected units creating an impression of continuous flow. Either of the two designs may be arranged as continuing motifs simply by placing them end-to-end, making overlapping connections where indicated by the dotted lines.

In the section entitled Design Units (pages 132-183) you will find these and other flowers, leaves and berries, with descriptions of stitch patterns and suggestions as to colors.

These five individual units are adaptable to a variety of decorative uses in the form of belts, luggage straps, bell pulls, curtains, sweaters, borders for envelope handbags, eyeglass cases, pincushions, etc.

A

B

C

D

E

113

(*Top left*) An envelope bag, with zippered closing. *Embroidered by Mrs. John F. Jewett, Needham, Mass.*

(*Top right*) A pouch-type bag with a full design, finished with frame and handle. *Embroidered by Mrs. Harold C. Urschel, Chestnut Hill, Mass.*

(*Left*) A pouch-type bag, with a simple leaf motif, finished with frame and handle. *Embroidered by Mrs. John L. Porter, Randolph, Mass.*

(*Bottom left*) Another envelope bag, with zippered closing, tassel. *Embroidered by Mrs. John L. Porter, Randolph, Mass.*

(*Bottom right*) Another decorated pouch-type bag, finished with frame and handle. *Embroidered by Mrs. Robert Allen, East Walpole, Mass.*

114

(*Top*) Linen belt with floral motif. *Embroidered by Mrs. Robert Allen, East Walpole, Mass.*

(*Center*) Sweater with flower sprays. *Embroidered by Mrs. John S. Mason, Montclair, N. J.*

(*Center right*) Cardigan jacket with embroidered edging. *Embroidered by Mrs. John L. Porter, Randolph, Mass.*

(*Bottom left*) Dress with embroidery outlining neckline. *Embroidered by Mrs. John L. Porter, Randolph, Mass.*

116

(*Facing page, far left*) Bible cover. *Embroidered by Mrs. Arthur H. Sanford, Walpole, Mass.*

(*Facing page, bottom*) Covers for telephone directories. *Embroidered by the author.*

(*Facing page, left*) Tasseled bellpull. *Embroidered by Mrs. Allen E. Rosenberg, Chestnut Hill, Mass.*

Detail of bellpull shown on facing page. *Embroidered by Mrs. Allen E. Rosenberg, Chestnut Hill, Mass.*

(*Below*) Fire screen. *Embroidered by Mrs. Richard H. Sweet, Sullivan, N. H.*

(*Facing page*)

(*Top*) Design for a framed picture, which incorporates 40 different stitches. *Embroidered by Mrs. William R. Waddell, Denver, Colo.*

(*Center*) An arrangement of flowers and leaves, designed for use as a framed picture. *Embroidered by Mrs. Willard R. Kitchen, East Walpole, Mass.*

(*Bottom*) Another design, which also contains 40 different stitches. *Embroidered by Mrs. John F. Jewett, Needham, Mass.*

(*Left*) Wheat was chosen as the motif for a wall hanging made especially for the University of Iowa. *Courtesy Arthur H. Lee & Sons, Inc., Birkenhead, England, and New York.*

(*This page*)

A three-piece chair set. *Embroidered by Miss Mabel Everett, Walpole, Mass.*

Two complementary designs for a pair of framed pictures. *Embroidered by Mrs. Harry Gordon, Brookline, Mass.*

(*This page*)

Large wall hanging. *Embroidered by Mrs. Clifford S. Jones, Brookline, Mass.*

(*Facing page*)

A pair of designs for mounting in oval frames. *Embroidered by Mrs. William R. Waddell, Denver, Colo.*

Portfolio cover. *Embroidered by the author.*

120

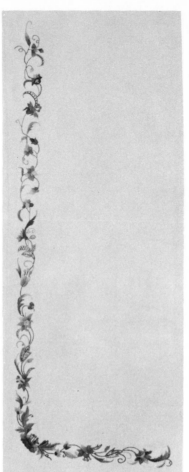

122

(From left to right, facing page)

A curtain with a floral border design. *Embroidered by Mrs. Arthur Jones, Walpole, Mass.*

A curtain with a narrow floral border. *Embroidered by Mrs. Robert Allen, East Walpole, Mass.*

Another curtain, with a design of flowers, leaves, berries and acorns. *Embroidered by Mrs. John L. Porter, Randolph, Mass.*

Cover for a footstool. *Embroidered by Mrs. Osborne Howes, Chestnut Hill, Mass.*

Another cover for a footstool. *Embroidered by Mrs. Willard R. Kitchen, East Walpole, Mass.*

(This page)

Detail of floral motif from a tablecloth. *Embroidered by Mrs. Arthur Colburn, Walpole, Mass.*

(Bottom left) Wing chair with back and sides of dark green velvet, with embroidery on panel of linen twill. *Embroidered by Mrs. William Williams, Walpole, Mass.*

(Bottom right) Wing chair. *Embroidered by Mrs. Richard H. Sweet, Sullivan, N. H.*

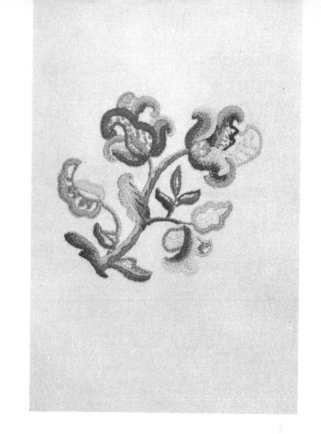

123

(*Facing page*)

Wall arrangement of pictures, including arrangement designed and embroidered by the author, shown in color on the jacket of this book and following page 132. *Embroidered by the author.*

Embroidered bedspread and canopy drop. *Courtesy E. Jay Rousuck; New York Arthritis and Rheumatism Foundation.*

(*This page*)

Bellpull with tassel. *Embroidered by Mrs. Everett W. Moxon, Falmouth, Mass.*

Interior of a house in the American Southwest, with a framed panel of a collector's piece of antique English crewel embroidery (featuring a Tree of Life design) hung over the fireplace. *Photograph by Maynard Parker, Courtesy House Beautiful. Embroidery from Elinor Merrill.*

Draperies and cushion-covers. *Embroidered by Mrs. Richard H. Sweet, Sullivan, N. H.*

Decorated workbag. *Courtesy* McCall's Needlework & Crafts Magazine.

(*Facing page*)

Decorative acorn trees have been embroidered and framed for an interesting wall decoration. *Courtesy* McCall's Needlework & Crafts Magazine.

126

(*This page*)

(*Bottom left*) Upholstered armchair, completely covered with embroidery. *Courtesy Arthur H. Lee & Sons, Inc., Birkenhead, England, and New York.*

(*Center*) Draperies embroidered in an all-over design. *Embroidered by Mrs. James Gilmore, Walpole, Mass.*

(*Facing page, right*) Draperies embroidered in a monochrome floral design. *Library of Mr. and Mrs. Gustave L. Levy; interior by Edward M. Benesch, A.I.D. Photograph by Alexandre Georges. Courtesy Interiors, © 1962, Whitney Publications, Inc.; New York Arthritis and Rheumatism Foundation.*

128

(*Below, left*) Victorian chair, embroidered on a background of dark green linen. *Embroidered by Mrs. Axel Anderson, Walpole, Mass.*

(*Below, right*) Armchair with embroidered chair-seat. *Owned by the author.*

(*Facing page, top left*) Side chair, with embroidered diamond pattern on chair-seat. *Embroidered by Mrs. Theodore Bennett, Chestnut Hill, Mass.*

(*Facing page, top right*) Side chair, with lyre back. *Embroidered by Mrs. Osborne Howes, Chestnut Hill, Mass.*

(*Facing page, bottom left*) Side chair with curved back. *Embroidered by Mrs. Osborne Howes, Chestnut Hill, Mass.*

(*Facing page, bottom right*) Side chair with upholstered seat. *Embroidered by Mrs. Bertram R. Paley, Chestnut Hill, Mass.*

CHAPTER SIX

DESIGN UNITS

THE individual elements—leaves, stems, tendrils, flowers, fruits and animals—which make up the familiar designs of crewel embroidery are the bits of magic that skillful fingers can weave into enchanting, jewel-like compositions. Many blossoms, birds and beasts amid the luxuriant foliage have no real counterparts; in fact, nature is sometimes drab by comparison.

The collection of design units shown on these pages cannot begin to encompass all the imaginative creations developed by embroiderers through the centuries. But it is representative of the wondrously-patterned units most frequently found in traditional crewel embroidery designs and provides the means of creating your own future heirlooms.

These design units should not be regarded as a formidable subject to be mastered only by hours of disciplined study but rather as a source of unending inspiration and delight. Do browse at will, picking up a detail here and there that interests you.

There are no inflexible rules governing the choice of stitches or colors. Some stitches are more adaptable to certain situations or requirements than others. Sometimes three or four stitches are equally suitable, and these are presented as alternative choices: for instance, knot, stem, outline or chain. Do not let such specific suggestions close the door to other attractive possibilities. If you feel in the mood to experiment with still other stitches, by all means do so.

The same is true of colors. Shades of green and brown are usually utilized for stems, tendrils, branches and tree trunks, with grey and browns the usual choice for animals. In the case of flowers and leaves, however, the imagination may soar freely, and often does. The notations which accompany the drawings and directions may suggest a set of value sequences or leave the actual color selections to you. Color directions may occasionally be given in this fashion: #1 brown, #2 blue, #2 and #3 bright green. In such cases it is intended that these colors be used in the exact sequences given: that is, brown in value #1, then blue in value #2, followed by bright green in value #2 and, finally, bright green in value #3.

For ready reference within the text and elsewhere, each individual design unit included here has been numbered, from Design Unit 1 to Design Unit 156. There are also composite designs, Design I to Design VI.

There are also a number of small units without explanatory text which serve as attractive space-fillers and also add to the total number of design units available. It is hoped that you will want to return again and again to this crewel storehouse to find inspiration for many lovely interpretations of your own.

TREE-TRUNKS AND BRANCHES

When a tree is the central unit in a design, it must be handled skillfully, for by its size and position it can easily dominate the scene unless its background role, supporting and pulling the entire design together, is clearly defined. Here placement of color is the primary key, with stitch patterns following close behind.

Tree-trunk colors are best kept quiet and subdued, so that they blend unobtrusively into the harmonic background of the piece, give it depth and substance and create pleasing contrasts to the dominant and accent colors.

Trunks and branches are essentially blends of browns and greens of matching intensities; that is, #3 brown against #3 green, #4 brown against #4 green, etc. The brown-green values should be graded from dark at the base toward medium in the upper branches, starting, for example, at the bottom with #5 or #4 and working up through #3 or #2.

An effective finishing touch is to bring the flower colors—the reds, the golds, the blues—directly into the trunks and branches through the use of small outline stitches intermingled at random among the basic greens and browns. This is a subtle and charming way to pull the whole color scheme together. Flowers or leaves which rest on or lie across portions of a tree should be worked in colors which contrast with the basic tree colors.

Many stitches are adaptable to tree-trunks. Outline and stem stitches are particularly suitable for the color-blending techniques suggested. One color may be accented over another color of the same intensity by judicious stitch selection. For instance, chain stitches have more bulk than outline stitches; therefore colors will stand out more prominently in chain stitches than in outline stitches.

The tree trunk in this design was closely worked in small outline stitches. The darker values of green and brown were carefully chosen to be of matching intensities. Values of #5, #4 and #3 were worked from the base of the tree toward the top. Note how the medium values of flower and leaf colors are intermingled here with the basic browns and greens. They are used generously and spaced at irregular intervals. The whole effect is designed to create a subtle infusion of harmonic colors as a chromatic background to the whole picture. Incidentally, the full-sized framed picture actually measures 20 x 30 inches.

TENDRILS, STEMS AND BRANCHES

Design Unit 1

Chain, twisted chain, or knot, worked closely.

Design Unit 2

Outline, or heavy stem, worked closely, side by side.

Design Unit 3

Open, or spaced buttonhole, with value #3 on one side, #4 on the other.

Design Unit 4

Closed buttonhole, with value #3 on one side, #4 on the other.

Design Unit 5

Knot, outline, thorn (fern). The knot stitch is best for maintaining contours of tendrils that vary in size and shape. Where tendrils thicken use satin stitches as filler.

Note: Colors suggested are greens or browns, or combinations of both. For most effective results with stems and branches arrange color gradations from light on one side to dark on the other.

Design Unit 6

Satin stitches arranged in blocks (here called brick stitches) make beautiful and effective fillers for large branches and trunks. Start along the outside edge of the trunk with a series of alternating long and short bricks running from top to bottom, as used along the right edge of the diagram below: Then, make a series of long bricks (the dotted bricks). Finish with shorter bricks where necessary to complete the trunk, as along the left edge. Fit the bricks snugly against each other.

Count the stitches in your first brick and make all additional bricks conform, so that the effect will be uniform. However, you may easily add a stitch if needed in going around a curve. The trunk shown here is two bricks wide. Trunks may, of course, be wider or smaller than this. Brick-stitch filling is easier and more attractive if you assure uniformity by outlining in pencil the brick rectangles you intend to fill.

Use three values (#3, #4, #5) of browns and greens, starting with the darkest value at the base and working upward. Branches and stems which veer off from the trunk can be worked in outline stitches, using the same general colors as in the trunk.

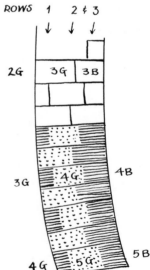

LAID WORK FOR STEMS AND BRANCHES

Design Unit 7
Laid work in #4 brown, tied with *open* chain stitches in #3 green.

Design Unit 8
Laid work in #3 green, tied by whipped (overcast) stitches in #3 brown.

Design Unit 9
Laid work in color of your selection, held by irregular scattered seeds in a contrasting color. Be sure the seeds tie all strands of the laid work.

Design Unit 10
Laid work in color of your selection, held by tiny running (darning) stitches in a contrasting color.

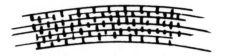

Design Unit 11
Laid work in color of your selection, held by detached fly stitches in a contrasting color.

Design Unit 12
Laid work in color of your selection, held by couching threads that form varying arrangements, illustrated below.

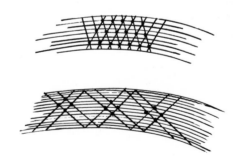

Notes covering laid work and couching in some detail are found in the section on stitches (pages 108-109).

135

MOUNDS

Small mounds, or hillocks, often appear at the base of designs which feature a tree as the central motif. Occasionally these have small plants, flowers, leaves or animals nestled in them. The mounds may be made to appear heavy or light in texture, depending upon the pattern and upon personal inclination. The four mound designs shown here vary in texture from heavy to light. Stitch patterns may be varied to create a variety of mounds when several are used in a single pattern. In most of the older crewel pieces long and short stitches were used lavishly in the filling of mounds. Modern usage suggests a more varied stitchery.

Mound colors are mostly greens and browns, with some golds and deep blues, all used with careful attention to value sequences. Excellent green-brown combinations may be chosen from the first two rows of the color chart.

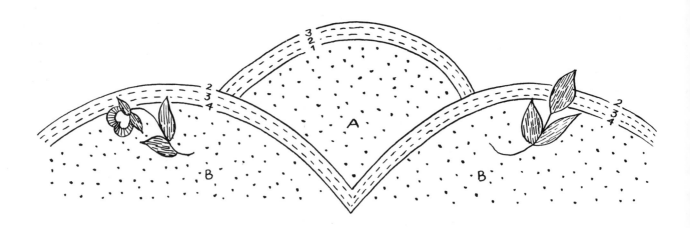

Design Unit 13

A. Chain, outline, knot, or twisted chain, worked closely. Top row colors are #3 brown, #2 green and #1 green. Fill remainder of mound with irregular seed stitches in #3 brown.

B. Stitch selections as in A. Top-row colors are #2 green, #3 green and #4 brown. Fill with irregular seed stitches in #3 or #4 brown.

The leaf and flower units should be made in colors harmonizing with those used in the pattern. Make these two units before filling with seed stitches.

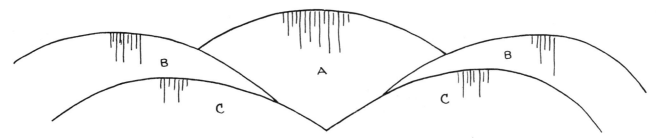

Design Unit 14 △

These mounds are entirely filled with long and short stitches, affording an excellent opportunity to experiment with mixing and blending colors. Use the same colors and values planned for the rest of the pattern. One color-grouping could be:

A. #5 green
    #5 olive green
    #4 old blue
    #4 blue green
    #4 green
B. #1 golden brown
    #1 green
    #3 green
    #4 old blue
C. #2 brown
    #1 bright green
    #3 bright green
    #3 green
    #4 green

Design Unit 15

A. Begin with three rows of knot stitches: top row, #2 green; middle row, #3 green; bottom row, #4 brown. Fill remainder of mounds with small wheat ears in #3 green, completing them with small back stitches in #4 brown.
B. Long and short. Start at top with #1 brown and work toward bottom, successively using #2 brown, #2, #3, #4 green and #4 brown.
C. Herringbone in bands at top, using #3 green tied with #4 brown. Work edges of bands in outline stitch, using #3 brown. Fill remainder of mounds with irregular seed stitches in #3 or #4 green.

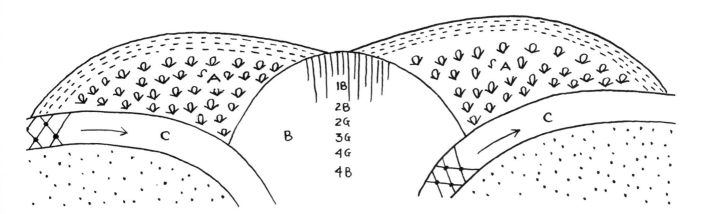

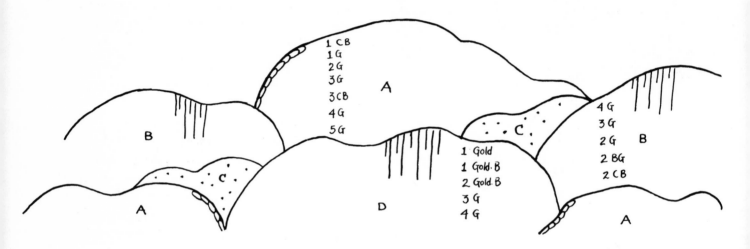

Design Unit 16

A. Chain stitch. Follow color suggestions on drawing, successively using #1 chocolate brown, #1, #2 and #3 green, #3 chocolate brown, #4 and #5 green.

B. Long and short. Start at top with #4 green, and work toward bottom, successively using #2 green, #2 bright green and #2 chocolate brown.

C. Small irregular seed stitches in #3 or #4 brown.

D. Long and short, successively using #1 gold, #1 and #2 golden brown, #3 and #4 green.

SMALL LEAVES

PITMAN

Many embroiderers are seemingly unaware of the color and stitch possibilities in the treatment of small leaves. These, along with tendrils, are excellent space-fillers. Just because they are small, do not dismiss them casually. Whenever possible use two color values, and at least two stitches, within each individual leaf. You can use even greater variety if the leaf is adaptable to it. Also try to vary the color and stitch patterns from leaf to leaf in outlining, shading, veining, etc. Small leaves of identical size and shape can be developed into completely individual units in this way. The cumulative effect of an imaginative approach to small leaves will be well worth the little added effort.

Arboreal motifs are usually worked in greens, but they need not be monotonous on this account. In most patterns you can use two families of greens; do so by all means.

Design Unit 17
Satin stitch, in values #1, #2 or #3.

Design Unit 18
Cretan stitch, in values #1, #2 or #3.

Design Unit 19
Buttonhole, in values #1, #3 or #4.

Design Unit 20
A.   Outline stitch in #2 green.
B.   French knots in #3 of a contrasting color.

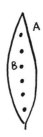

Design Unit 21
A.   Outline or knot in #3 green.
B.   Running stitch in #2 or #4 green.

139

Design Unit 22

A. Twisted chain in #4 green.
B. Seed in #3 or #4 of a contrasting color.

Design Unit 23

A. Chain in #2 green.
B. Chain in #3 green.
C. Seed in #3 or #4 of a contrasting color.

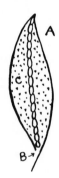

Design Unit 24

A. Attached fly in #3 or #4.
B. Outline stitch in #2 or #3.

Design Unit 25

A. Chain in #3 green.
B. Detached fly in #4 green, worked into the chain. Small back stitches in #4 of a contrasting color.

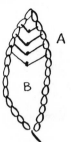

Design Unit 26

A. Bullion stitch in #3 green.
B. Edge leaf in chain or knot, using #2 or #4 green.

Design Unit 27

A. Outline stitch in #3 green.
B. Edge leaf in twisted chain, using #4 green. Center vein whipped (overcast) in a contrasting color.

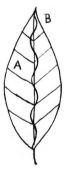

Design Unit 28

A. Couch in #2 or #3 green, tie with #4 of a contrasting color.

B. Satin stitch in #3 or #4 green.

Design Unit 29

A. Buttonhole in #3 green.

B. Satin in #2 green.

C. Vein: outline stitch in #4 of a contrasting color.

D. French knots in #3 gold.

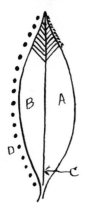

Design Unit 30

A. Buttonhole in #3 green.

B. French knots in #3 or #4 of a contrasting color.

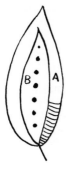

Design Unit 31

A. Open inverted buttonhole in #4 green (spokes of buttonhole fan out on outside edge).

B. Cross stitch in #3 green, or a contrasting color.

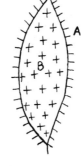

Design Unit 32

A. Knot in #2 green.

B. Buttonhole in #3 green.

C. Lazy daisy in #4 of a contrasting color.

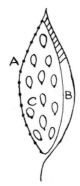

Design Unit 33

A. Attached wheat ears in #3 green; tie loop ends with small back stitches in #4 of a contrasting color.

B. Chain or knot stitch in #4 green.

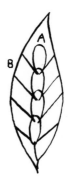

141

Design Unit 34

A. Chain, knot or outline, using gradations of green.
B. Edge leaf in twisted chain, #3 green.
C. Seed stitch in #4 or #5 of a contrasting color.

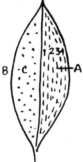

Design Unit 35

A. Open feather stitch (spread stitches slightly) in #4 green.
B. Edge leaf in knot stitch, #3 green.
C. French knots in #4 or #5 of a contrasting color.

Design Unit 36

Gradations of outline or chain stitches, running from light to dark.

Design Unit 37

A. Buttonhole in #4 green.
B. Wavy (zig zag) chain in #3 green.
C. Chain stitch in #2 green.

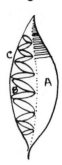

Design Unit 38

A. Gradations of outline stitch, light to dark.
B. Chain stitch in #3 green.
C. Detached fly stitch in a contrasting color; tie center of fly in #4 green.

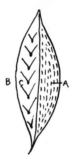

Design Unit 39

A. Buttonhole stitch inverted so edge is in leaf center; use #3 green.
B. Spaced loop stitch, #2 green.
C. French knots in #3 of a contrasting color.

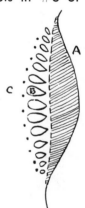

Design Unit 40

A. Outline leaf with one row of chain stitches in #3 olive green.

B. Stars in #3 gold, tie in #3 green if desired.

C. Long and short. Start at tip and work to base, using #1 gold, #1, #2, #3, #4 olive green.

Design Unit 41

A. Attached buttonhole in #2 aqua green.

B. Attached buttonhole in #3 aqua green.

C. Seed stitch in #3 old gold.

D. Cretan stitch in #4 aqua green.

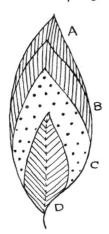

Design Unit 42

A. Double chain in #3 green.

B. Herringbone in #4 green, tied with #4 rust or rose.

C. Outline stitch around edges in #3 green.

D. Loop stitch in #4 or #5 rust or rose.

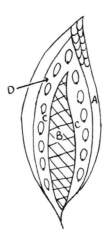

Design Unit 43

A. Couch center in #3 or #4 khaki; tie with #3 gold.

B. Buttonhole in #2 khaki.

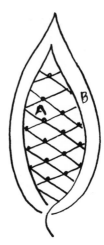

Design Unit 44

A. Buttonhole or satin stitch in #4 bright green.

B. Knot stitch in #3 bright green.

C. Loop stitches in #4 rust, tied at one end with #3 bright green.

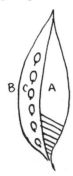

Design Unit 45

A. Twisted chain in #3 blue green.

B. Wheat ears in #3 old gold.

C. Satin stitch in #3 blue green.

D. French knots in #4 old gold.

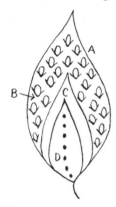

Design Unit 46

A. Edge leaf in chain stitch, using #3 green.

B. Spaced attached buttonhole in #2 green.

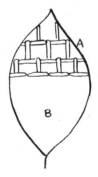

Design Unit 47

Laid work in #3 green, tied with scattered seed stitches in #3 or #4 of a contrasting color.

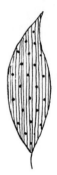

Design Unit 48

Laid work in #3 or #4 green. Anchor with detached fly stitches in #3 of a contrasting color.

144

Design Unit 49
Laid work in #4 green. Couch in #2 or #3 green and tie in #4 of a contrasting color.

Design Unit 50
Laid work in #4 golden brown. Tie with small attached fly stitches in #3 green.

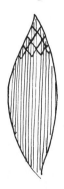

Design Unit 51
Laid work in #3 chocolate brown. Tie with small running stitches in #3 or #4 green.

Design Unit 52
Leaf Combinations.
A. Leaf #48 in blue greens.
B. Chain stitch in gradations of green from light edges to dark center.
C. Outline leaf with yellow green chain stitches; fill leaf with closely worked irregular running stitches.
D. Leaf #50 in blue greens.
E. Twisted chain, with yellow green gradations from light on one side of leaf to dark on the other.
F. Outline stitch, in green gradations from light to dark.
G. Leaf #47.

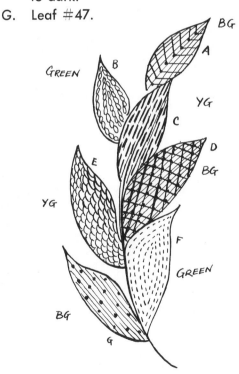

145

MEDIUM LEAVES

PITMAN

Medium-sized leaves offer an expanded scope for the embroiderer in color and stitch possibilities. There is usually enough area within individual leaves to make effective use of various couching and filling stitches. Here you may find interesting employment for the four types of trellis couchings (pages 85, 108), and for fly, wheatear, arrowhead, seed and other similar decorative stitches.

The suggestions made in the following group of design units are but a few of the combinations of colors and stitches that can be used attractively. These somewhat larger leaves afford an opportunity to use colors other than shades of green much more effectively than in the case of small leaves. When working in the conventional arboreal greens, be sure to introduce two families whenever the design size permits. Some excellent pairings of colors are suggested in the chapter on Color Planning (pages 62-63).

Design Unit 53

A. Attached fly, or open Cretan stitch in #3 green.
B. Satin stitch in #2 green.
C. Chain stitch in #4 green.

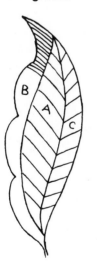

Design Unit 54

"Scale" filling, using buttonhole stitch in green gradations in a scalloped formation. Edge leaf in outline stitches, using #3 green.

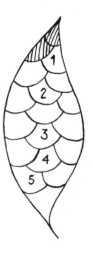

Design Unit 55

A. Couch in #3 and #4 greens; tie in #4 of a contrasting color.

B. Edge leaf in outline stitch, using #2 green.

Design Unit 56

A. Couch in #3 and #4 green; tie with #3 or #4 of a contrasting color.

B. Edge leaf in chain stitch, using #3 green.

C. Buttonhole in #2 green.

D. French knots in #2 of a contrasting color.

E. One row of outline stitch in #4 green.

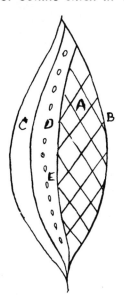

Design Unit 57

A. Long and short, using #3, #4 and #5 golden brown.

B. Solid chain stitch. Work from outside to center, using #1 brown, #1, #2, #3 and #4 green.

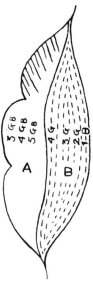

Design Unit 58

Laid work in #4 or #5 old gold; couching in #3 or #4 green, tied with #4 green. Edge leaf with stem stitches in #3 green, then finish with outside rows of French knots in #3 old gold.

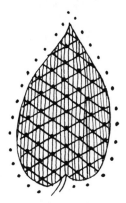

Design Unit 59

A. Buttonhole stitch in #4 green on one side, #3 green on the opposite.

B. Detached wheat ear in #3 of a contrasting color, with extra fly stitch under wheat ears in #4 green.

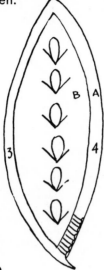

Design Unit 60

A. Edge the leaf with two rows of chain, or twisted chain, in #2 or #3 green. Whip (overcast) the two rows of chain in #3 or #4 of a contrasting color.

B. Seed stitch or French knots in #3 of a contrasting color.

C. Vein in outline stitch, using #4 green.

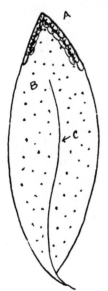

Design Unit 61

A. Open chain in #4 green.

B. Outline stitch in #4 green.

C. Outline stitch in #3 green, with French knots at each point in #3 or #4 of a contrasting color.

Design Unit 62

A. Satin or buttonhole in #2 green.

B. Rumanian stitch in #3 green.

C. Seed stitch in #4 of a contrasting color.

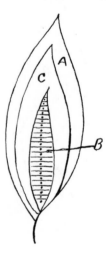

Design Unit 63
Satin stitches in #3 and #5 following diagram for stitch directions. A vein of a contrasting color may be added after satin stitches are completed.

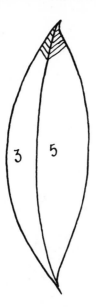

Design Unit 64
A. Solid chain from outside edge to center, using #1, #2, #3, and #4 olive green, #4 and #5 golden brown.
B. Long and short, beginning at outside edge with #1 golden brown, followed by #2 and #3 golden brown, #4 olive green.

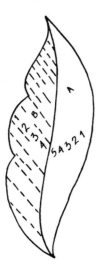

Design Unit 65
A. Herringbone in #3 blue green, tied in #4 brick.
B. Outline stitch in #2 blue green.
C. Attached buttonhole in #2 blue green.
D. Attached buttonhole in #3 blue green.
E. Seed stitch in #5 brick.

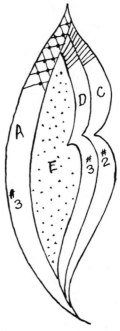

Design Unit 66
A. Double chain stitch in #2 blue green.
B. Attached buttonhole in light to dark gradations of blue green.
C. Fill with small sheaf (fagot) stitches in #3 old gold.

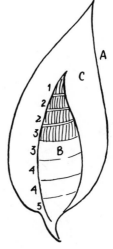

149

Design Unit 67

A. Double chain or closed herringbone in #3 chocolate brown.

B. Closely worked outline stitches in green gradations from light edge to dark center.

C. Seed stitch in #3 green.

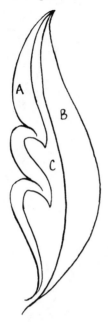

Design Unit 68

A. Buttonhole stitch in #2 green.

B. Satin stitch in #2 green.

C. Satin stitch in #3 green.

D. Seed stitch in #3 old gold.

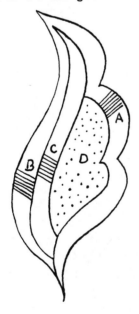

Design Unit 69

A. Fill with chevron stitches *worked closely* in #2 aqua green. The stitch will form its own outline.

B. Repeat, using #3 aqua green.

C. Use any filling stitch in #4 of a contrasting color.

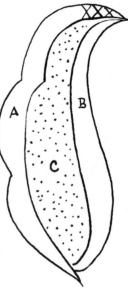

Design Unit 70

A. Long and short, working from outside edge to center with #3, #4 and #5 brown.

B. Solid chain stitches, working from outside edge to center with #1 brown, followed by #1, #2 and #3 green.

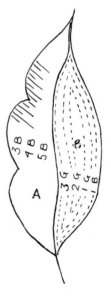

Design Unit 71

A. Two rows of chain in #3 and #2 green.
B. Any small fill-in stitch in #3 of contrast.
C. Double chain in #2 green..
D. Seed stitch in #4 of contrast.
E. Knot stitch in #4 green.

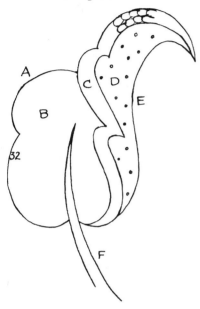

Design Unit 72

A. Satin stitch in #3 blue.
B. Long and short in green gradations as shown.

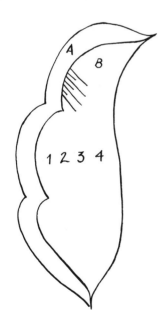

Design Unit 73

A. Long and short, using khaki and green values as shown.
B. Straight running stitches, using #3 khaki.

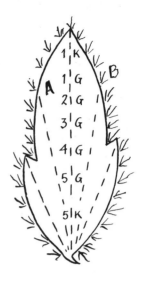

Design Unit 74

A. Satin stitch in #3 gold.
B. Satin stitch in #3 green.
C. Long and short, beginning at outside edge with #1 green, followed by #2 and #3 green, with #3 gold nearest center.

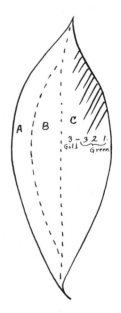

151

Design Unit 76

A. Buttonhole stitch with any medium value of green.

B. Fill with small running or seed stitches in a contrasting color.

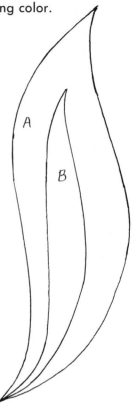

Design Unit 75

Long and short, beginning at tip with #1 khaki, followed by #1, #2, #3, #4 and #5 green, #5 khaki. When leaf is covered a vein may be worked over the long and short, using an outline stitch in #5 khaki.

LEAF SPRAY

Design Unit 77

Leaf Spray. Up to this point, a good many different leaf treatments have been illustrated (#17—#76). This simple 20-leaf spray affords an interesting opportunity to practice a variety of stitch combinations and to create an attractive and useful crewel piece at the same time. You might want to use a different pattern for each leaf—all 20 of them! The design is quite simple, yet could be most effective on a sweater, a skirt or other apparel, a handbag or perhaps made into a pair of pictures.

Colors: You might want to use combinations from either Row 1 or Row 2 of the color chart. Don't forget those ever-so-important accent touches.

152

153

LARGE LEAVES

Part of a bed curtain, worked in crewels on cotton-and-linen twill, made in New England, probably Massachusetts, 1700-1725. *Courtesy Museum of Fine Arts, Boston, Mass.*

Large leaves present a challenge to any embroiderer. When properly done they can be outstandingly attractive. The possibilities for combinations of pleasing colors and stitches are so varied you may be tempted to let your virtuosity carry you beyond the bounds of artistic desirability. Thus, a word of caution so that you may achieve a balanced effect.

The large areas within such leaves do provide excellent opportunities for the use of couching, especially battlemented couching, as well as laid work. But balance both of these by rather generous use of regular filling stitches. Do not permit laid work or couching to become commonplace through overuse.

The veins in large leaves present an opportunity to employ your best skills in making them interesting. Here also you will find places to use the attached wheatear, fly, loop and other similar stitches.

Design Unit 78

A. Squared (overlaid) couching in #1, #2, #3 and #4 rust, tied with #4 olive green. Two sets of plain couching are placed so that the threads cross each other.

B. Long and short, working from the top to bottom edges, using #1 rust, then #1, #2, #3, #4 and #5 olive green.

C. Knot stitch in khaki gradations as shown.

D. One row of twisted chain in #3 olive green.

E. Long and short, with colors as in C above.

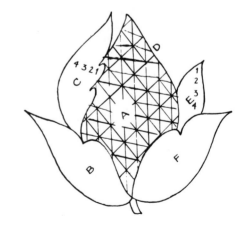

154

Design Unit 79

A. Couch in #2 and #3 aqua blue, tied in #3 old gold.

B. Stars in #3 gold, tied at center in #3 aqua blue.

C. Three rows of twisted chain in #1, #2 and #3 aqua blue.

D. One row of outline stitches in #4 aqua blue.

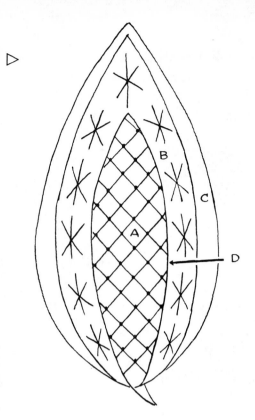

Design Unit 80

A. Couch in #2 and #3 green, tied in #4 of a contrasting color.

B. Knot stitch in #3 green.

C. Tiny outline stitches in #3 of contrast.

D. Attached buttonhole in #3 and #4 of contrast.

E. Long and short in green, with value sequences as in F below.

F. Fill solidly with knot stitches, using green value sequences shown.

Design Unit 81

A. The entire leaf is filled with long and short, using aqua blue, green and bright yellow green in value sequences indicated.

B. Veins are superimposed in #4 golden brown after completion of the long and short.

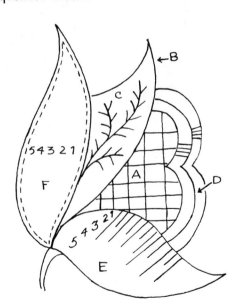

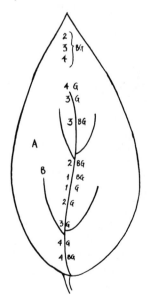

155

Design Unit 82

A. Long and short, beginning at tip of leaf and working to bottom, using #1, #2 bright green, then #1, #2, #3 and #4 gold as in drawing.

B. Veins in outline stitch in #4 brown.

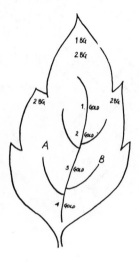

Design Unit 83

A. Outline the leaf in broad chain stitches, using #3 green on one side, #4 green on the other.

B. Laid work in #4 green, tied with detached fly stitches in #5 rust.

C. Detached fly stitches in #4 rust, tied in #3 green.

Design Unit 84

A. Cloud stitch. First, work small back stitches in #5 rose. Lace through these with #3 or #4 green.

B. Heavy chain in #3 green.

C. Long and short. Tip scalloped edge with #1 rose, then work to outer edge through #1, #2 and #3 green.

D. Twisted chain in #4 green.

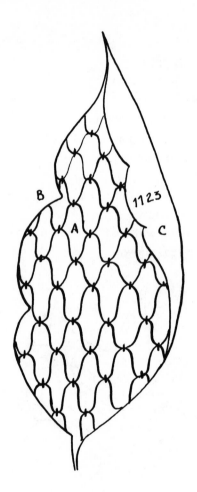

156

Design Unit 85

A. Fill solidly with knot stitches, using a gradation of greens.

B. Three rows of chain stitches around entire edge, using green values #3, #4 and #5, starting with #3 outside.

C. Solid satin stitches in gradations of rust or rose.

D. Small scattered seed stitches in #3 green.

Design Unit 86

A. Couch in #2 and #3 green. At lower corners anchor with three small satin stitches in #4 brick, as illustrated.

B. Chain stitch in #3 green, caught through center of each chain with small back stitches in #4 brick.

C. Repeat B, using #4 green and #5 brick.

D. Fill solidly with long and short stitches in green gradations tipped with #1 brick, as indicated.

E. One row of outline stitch in #4 green.

F. Loop stitches in #5 brick, tied with #4 green at one end of each loop.

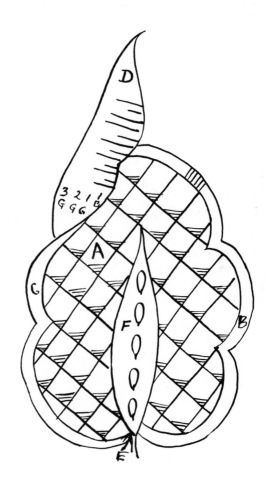

Design Unit 87

A. Chain stitch worked solidly in blue green value sequences as indicated.

B. Three rows of knot stitches placed close together, using blue greens #1, #2 and #3.

C. Fill with small seed stitches in #3 gold.

D. Vein in outline stitch, #4 gold.

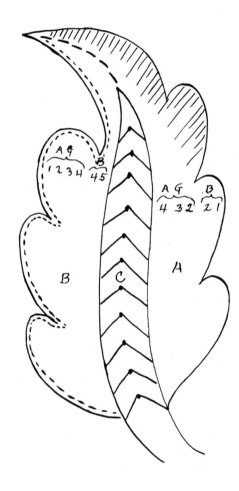

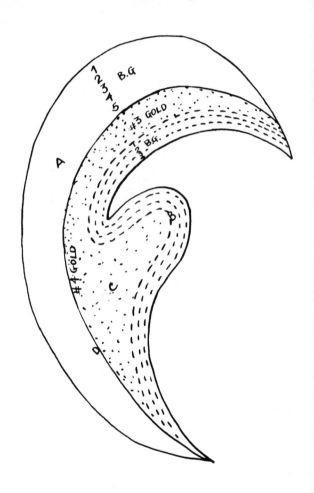

Design Unit 88

A. Long and short, working from outside edge toward center, using #1 and #2 brick, #2, #3 and #4 aqua green in sequence.

B. Solid chain, working from outside edge toward center, using #1, #2, #3 and #4 aqua green, #4 and #5 brick in sequence, as in drawing.

C. Inverted fly stitches in #5 aqua green, caught with extra back stitch in #5 brick.

158

Design Unit 89

A. Loop stitches arranged as indicated; use value #3 of any color.

B. As in A, using value #4.

C. As in A, using value #5.

D. Entire edge of leaf in outline stitch, using #4 green.

E. Fill with long and short, starting with values #1 and #2 of the color used in A, B and C, then working into gradations of green.

F. Seed stitches in #3 green.

Design Unit 90

A. Long and short, in #1, #2 and #3 green.

B. Heavy chain in #3 and #4 green.

C. Seeds in #3 green.

D. Flower in any colors you wish.

Design Unit 91

A. Long and short, in olive green and gold. Follow value sequences in drawing.

B. Long and short, in olive green and khaki. Follow value sequences in drawing.

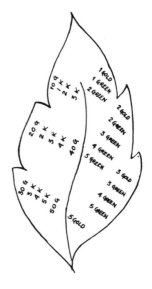

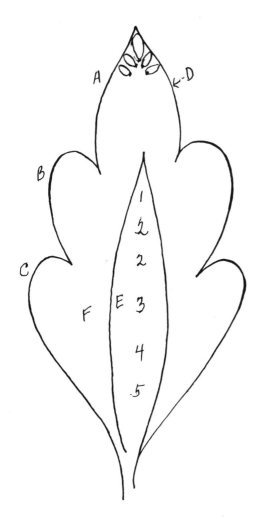

BERRIES AND ACORNS

PITMAN

Sprays, even whole trees, of various-sized berries and acorns, realistic and exotic, appear often in crewel embroidery designs. They not only afford an opportunity for color-balancing, but they are excellent space-fillers. Here is a fine medium for those brilliant little splashes of color you may have been waiting for. But *balance* them, please.

In addition to the conventional stitch patterns described in the eight small units immediately following, an interesting effect may be attained by adapting the spider-web technique to give a raised effect. The spider web stitch is described in some detail on page 90.

Design Unit 92

Do small berries in solid satin stitches or French knots. Value gradations from light at top to dark at bottom are most effective. Do leaves in greens, using Cretan, buttonhole or satin stitches.

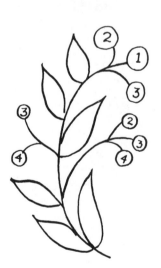

Design Unit 93

Medium-sized berries may be handled interestingly in two values of satin stitches, as indicated. Handle leaves as in Unit 92.

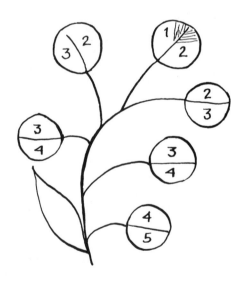

Design Unit 94

Large berries offer plenty of possibilities for stitch variety.

A. Chain stitch, worked closely. Value sequences, as shown.
B. Outline stitch with value sequences, as shown.
C. Leaves in harmonizing greens.

Design Unit 95

This is often referred to as a "fish eye" (inverted buttonhole). Fill the berry with satin stitches, then surround it with inverted open buttonhole stitches in a lighter value of the same, or contrasting, color. Do leaves in harmonizing greens.

Design Unit 96

Laid work in value #3 or #5. Couch with two lighter values of the same or a contrasting color. Tie couching with yarn of a definitely contrasting color.

Design Unit 97

A. Satin stitches, with contrasting French-knot center.
B. Buttonhole stitches, with contrasting satin-stitch center.
C. French knots, with contrasting French-knot center.

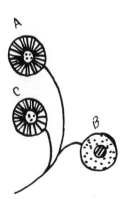

Design Unit 98

Acorn clusters may be worked in a variety of stitches, using harmonious browns and golds.

A. Cup: Solid French knots in medium to dark brown.
    Top: Buttonhole stitches in #2 and #3 gold.

B. Cup: Buttonhole in #4 or #5 brown.
    Top: Long and short in golds.

C. Cup: Bullion stitches in #4 or #5 brown.
    Top: Solid French knots in golds.

D. Cup: Laid work in #5 brown; couching in #2 and #3 brown, tied with #4 brown.
    Top: Satin stitches in #2 or #3 gold.

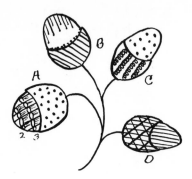

Design Unit 99

Larger acorns allow greater value-gradations, as illustrated here.

A. Cup: Long and short in #4 and #5 brown.
    Top: Long and short in #3, #2, #1 gold, going into #1 bright yellow green at the cup.

B. Cup: Follow directions for D of Unit 98.
    Top: Long and short, in gold values #1, #2 and #3.

Part of an embroidered curtain believed to have been made by members of the Wade family, Ipswich, Mass., 1725-1750. *Courtesy Museum of Fine Arts, Boston, Mass.*

162

OPEN-FACED FLOWERS

Courtesy Victoria & Albert Museum, Flowers in English Embroidery.

These versatile flowers, large and small, are found in great variety throughout crewel embroidery. The larger types are sometimes referred to as Tudor roses, and the smaller ones are said to be representative of the potato blossom which, in seventeenth-century England, still had an exotic aura of the New World about it.

These simple flowers may be easily wrought in so many stitch patterns that one's imagination is invited to run riot—and should. Use any color combinations you wish, but do make each petal stand out.

Design Unit 100

A. (Also B and C). Attached buttonhole stitches in value bands, as illustrated.

D. Seed stitches in values of a contrasting color.

E. Solid French knots in #3 or #4 of a contrasting color. In order to make French knots stand out against the surrounding seeds, circle this section with one row of outline stitches in any pale green.

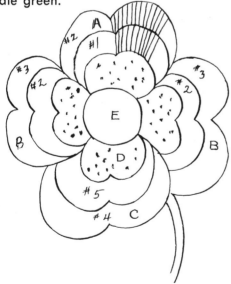

Design Unit 101

A. Stems: Fine outline stitches in #1 or #2 green. Tips: Satin stitch in #2 or #3 gold.

B. Long and short, working from tip to center, using values #1, #2 and #3 successively.

C. Repeat, with values #2, #3 and #4.

D. Repeat, with values #3, #4 and #5.

E. Satin stitch in value #3 of color in stamen tips. You may wish to vary this flower by working tiny seed stitches over the long and short in a contrasting color or, if you prefer, in value #5 of the same color. (See petal D.)

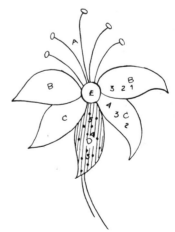

◁

Design Unit 103

A. Satin stitch outside band in value #1.
B. Repeat, using value #2.
C. Repeat, using value #3.
D. Seed stitch in values #2 or #3 of a contrasting color.
E. Long and short in values #1 and #2.
F. Repeat, with values #2 and #3.
G. Repeat, with values #3 and #4.
H. French knots in #3 of a contrasting color.

Design Unit 104

This flower is done in long and short, working from the outer edge toward bright yellow green all around the center.

A. Values #3, #2 and #1, into #1 bright yellow green.
B. Values #4, #3 and #2, into #1 bright yellow green.
C. Values #5, #4 and #3, into #2 bright yellow green.
D. French knots in #3 of a contrasting color.

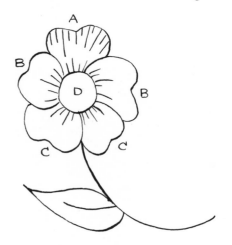

Design Unit 102

A. Buttonhole stitch outside band in value #2.
B. Repeat, using value #3.
C. Repeat, using value #4.
D. Repeat, using value #5.
E. Satin stitches in value #4 of a contrasting color.
F. Tiny scattered seed stitches in #2 or #3 of a contrasting color.

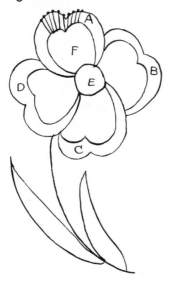

164

Design Unit 105

In this flower the couching should be done first.

A. Long and short, in values #1, #2 and #3, as illustrated.
B. Repeat, with values #2, #3 and #4.
C. Repeat, with values #3, #4 and #5.
D. Couch with #2 and #3 green, tie with #3 gold.
E. Solid satin stitch in #2 bright green.

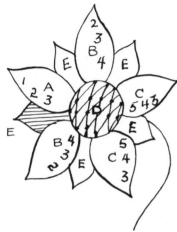

Design Unit 106

All petals of this flower are done in solid chain stitch.

A. Four or five value-gradations from light at the outer edge to dark in the center.
B. Repeat value gradations, with darkest value adjoining petal A to create a shadowed effect.
C. Repeat.
D. Repeat.
E. Satin stitches in #3 of a contrasting color.

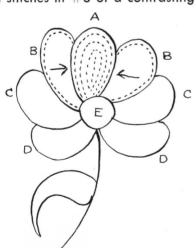

Design Unit 107

Some colors are suggested, others are of your choice. All petals of this flower are worked in herringbone and edged with outline stitch for a more finished appearance.

A. Value #2, tied in #3 of a contrasting color, edged in value #1.
B. Value #3, tied in #4 of a contrasting color, edged in value #2.
C. Value #4, tied in #5 of a contrasting color, edged in value #4.
D. May be treated as leaves, using Rumanian stitch in #3 green.
E. French knots in #3 of a contrasting color, with small underside crescent in satin stitch, using #2 green.

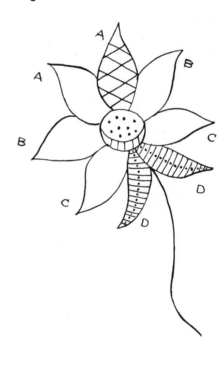

165

Design Unit 108

All solid satin stitches. Center in French knots, #3 gold.

A. *Value #1.*
B. Value #2.
C. Value #3.
D. Value #4.

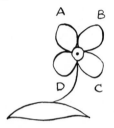

Design Unit 109

Couch center first, using #2 and #3 green. Tie with #3 gold. Petals in long and short, using blue and purple. Begin at outer edge and work toward center, with value sequences below:

A. #1, #2 and #3 blue, #3 purple.
B. #2, #3 and #4 blue, #4 purple.
C. #2, #3 and #4 purple, #4 blue.

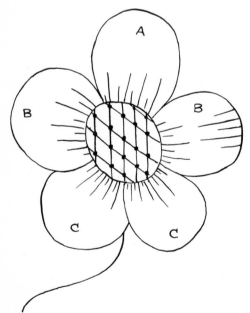

Design Unit 110

All solid Cretan stitches. Center in French knots in #3 of a contrasting color.

A. Value #1.
B. Value #2.
C. Value #4.
D. Value #5.
E. Value #3.

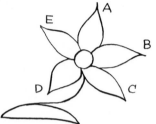

Design Unit 111

This spray is worked entirely in long and short. Colors of your selection, with value sequences as suggested in illustration. Centers in French knots in #3 or #4 of a contrasting color.

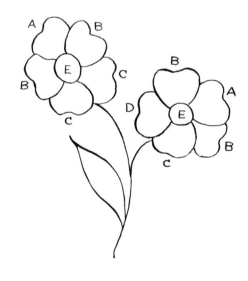

CARNATIONS, TULIPS, POMEGRANATES

These floral motifs are among the most interesting, colorful and versatile in crewel's garden. They are wonderfully adaptable to realistic or exotic treatment, in design, stitch pattern, color, or all three.

The carnation, once a symbol of the Stuarts, has been a favorite of embroiderers for generations. It is still enormously popular, and justly so; it can be enchanting. Tulip-like flowers were also much favored in old crewelwork patterns, and are adaptable to a variety of treatments. As your crewel techniques develop it will be an interesting challenge to see how many interpretations you can create. Exotic companions for tulip-like flowers are unusual leaves which bear a strong resemblance to tulips, some of which are illustrated below.

The pomegranate was a symbol of eternal life to many early embroiderers. It was a fruit introduced to England by intrepid voyagers. In its own right it can truly be characterized as exotic, while it lends itself easily to great versatility of treatment both in stitches and colors.

The suggestions given on the following pages are but an introduction to the multitude of possibilities open to the imaginative practitioner of the crewel art.

167

Design Unit 112

This flower may be done in 5-petal size (the C-D-E petals), or enlarged to include the A and B petals (in dotted outline). Description below covers the complete flower. All petals should be done in long and short. Color suggestions: Gold into green for contrast, using values #3, #2 and #1, completing with #1 of a contrasting color.

A. Work from outside edge to center, using values #3, #2 and #1, completing with #1 of a contrasting color.

B. Repeat with values #4, #3 and #2, completing with #2 of a contrasting color.

C. Repeat with values #1, #2, #3, #4 and #5. No contrast.

D. Repeat with values #2, #3, #4 and #5. No contrast.

E. Repeat A.

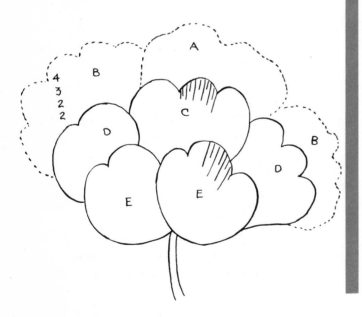

Design Unit 113

Colors of your selection.

A. Long and short. Work from outer edge toward center, using values #4, #3, #2 and #1.

B. Edge the petals with one row of outline stitches, then fill with small scattered seed stitches.

C. Repeat B.

D. Repeat A.

E. Cretan stitch in #3 green.

F. Satin stitch in #4 green.

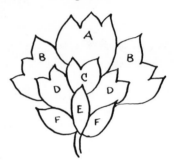

Design Unit 114

Colors of your selection.

A. Solid chain, working from outer edge to center, using values #1, #2, #3 and #4.

B. Solid knot stitches, repeating value sequences in A.

C. Repeat A.

D. Attached buttonhole stitch, using values #3 and #4.

E. Long and short, working from tip to base with values #1, #2, #3, #4 and #5.

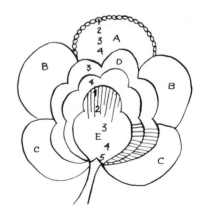

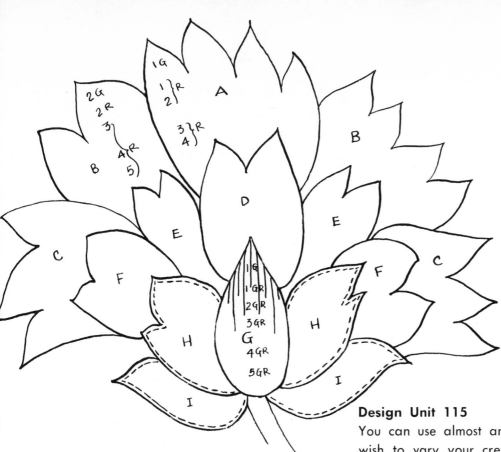

Design Unit 115

You can use almost any stitches and colors you wish to vary your crewel carnations. Long and short stitches lend themselves admirably to blending of colors in subtle combinations. Blue carnations tipped with purple and gold are lovely. In this design gradations of rust tipped with gradations of gold are suggested. Value sequences are varied in a way to give added interest to the petals and leaves. All petals are done in long and short. Leaves are worked in greens.

A. Tip with #1 gold, then work toward center with rust #1, #2, #3 and #4.

B. Repeat, with #2 gold at tip, then #2, #3, #4 and #5 rust.

C. Tip with #2 rust, then work toward center with rust #3, #4 and #5.

D. Five gradations of rust, starting with #1 at the tip.

E. Repeat colors and gradations in D.

F. Repeat colors and gradations in B.

G. Long and short. Tip with #1 gold, then work through green gradations, as illustrated.

H. Solid chain stitch, using all values of green.

I. Solid knot stitch, using all values of green.

169

Design Unit 116

Worked entirely in long and short.

A. Begin at the top edge with #1 gold, then work toward the base, using #1, #2, #3, #4 and #5 rose, with #5 golden brown at the base.

B. Repeat, omitting the golden brown.

C. Repeat B.

D. Note change in stitch direction. Use five values of rose, from #1 at the tip to #5 at the base.

Brick may be substituted for rose if you wish. Separation of petals may be emphasized by working one row of outline stitches in #5 golden brown along the dotted lines, as shown in the illustration.

Design Unit 117

A. Squared couching. (See Design Unit 78, page 154.) Use #3 and #4 purple for bottom layer; #2 and #1 purple for the top layer; tie with #3 green.

B. Long and short, with stitch direction as in A, Unit 116. Begin at the top edge and work to base, using #1 bright yellow green, #1 gold, #1, #2, #3, #4 and #5 purple, #5 rose at the base.

C. Solid chain stitches. Begin at outside edges and work in direction of arrows, using #1, #2, #3, #4 and #5 purple.

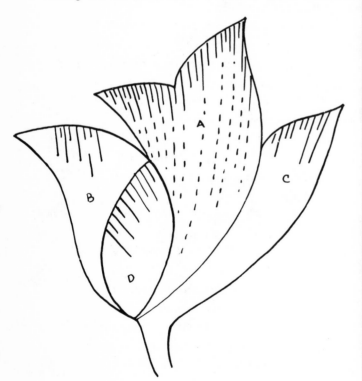

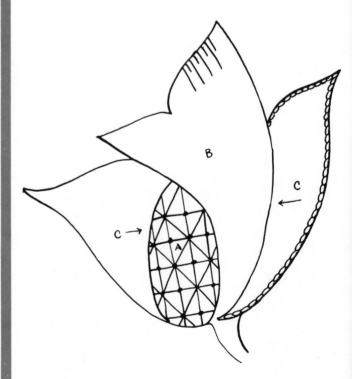

Design Unit 118

A. Laid work in #4 rust, tied with #3 green.

B. Satin stitches in #3 green.

C. One row of outline stitches in #3 rust worked closely around outside edge of B.

D. Long and short, beginning at top edge and working to base, using #1 gold, #1, #2, #3, #4 and #5 rust, #5 golden brown at the base.

E. Solid chain or knot stitches, starting at outside edge and working in direction of arrows with #1, #2, #3, #4 and #5 rust.

Design Unit 119

All in long and short except B.

A. Begin at top edge and work toward base, using #1 golden brown, #2 and #3 gold.

B. Couch in #2 and #3 golden brown, tie with #3 gold.

C. Begin at top edge and work toward base, using #2 golden brown, #2, #3, #4 and #5 gold, #5 golden brown.

D. As in A, using #1 golden brown, #2, #3 and #4 gold.

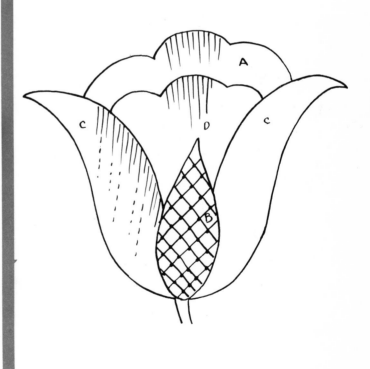

171

Design Unit 120

A. Couch in #2 and #3 chocolate brown, tie in #3 bright green.

B. Two rows of chain stitches in blue, value #3 outside, #2 inside.

C. Long and short. Begin at right edge of petal and work diagonally to other edge, using #1 blue, #1 brown, #1, #2, #3, #4 and #5 blue.

D. Long and short. Begin at top edge of petal and work diagonally to bottom edge, using #1 brown, #2 blue, #2, #3 and #4 bright green.

E. Chain stitch. Begin at outside edge and work in direction of arrow, using #1, #2, #3, #4 and #5 blue. Note changes in stitch direction.

Design Unit 121

A. Long and short. Begin at top edge and work to base, using #3, #2 rust, #2 and #1 gold, #1 yellow green.

B. Long and short. Color sequences similar to those in A, using #2 rust, #2 and #1 gold, #1 yellow green.

C. Herringbone in #3 olive green, tied with #4 gold. Run outline stitch around edges of petals in #4 olive green.

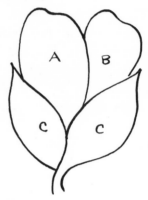

Design Unit 122

Your own color selections.

A. Buttonhole stitch in value #3.

B. Long and short. Begin at tip of petal and work toward base, using values #1, #2, #3, #4 and #5.

C. Solid chain stitch, worked from light to dark values in direction of arrows.

D. Scattered seed stitches in #1 or #2 of a contrasting color.

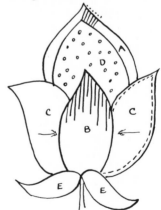

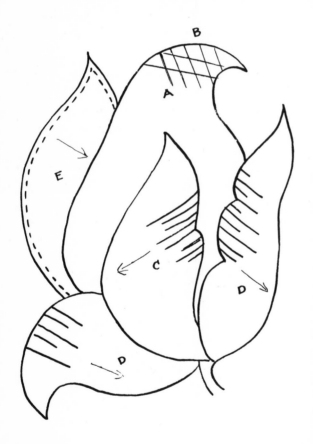

172

Design Unit 123

A. Long and short, working from top edge toward base, using #2 and #3 gold, #3 golden brown.

B. Repeat A, using #2, #3 and #4 gold, #4 golden brown. Emphasize separation of this petal by edging in outline stitch, #1 gold.

C. Solid chain, working from inner to outer edges, using #1, #2, #3, #4 and #5 olive green.

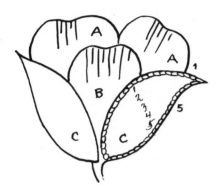

Design Unit 124

Stamen tips in satin stitch, #3 gold; stems in outline stitch, #1 bright green.

Petals in long and short, working from top edge to base, using #1 and #2 blue, #2 and #3 purple.

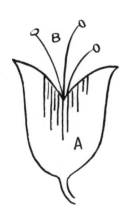

Design Unit 125

Long and short, in your own color selections. Work value sequences from top to bottom in one flower, reverse the order for the other flower.

Design Unit 126

Some colors suggested, others of your choice.

A. Long and short, starting at top edge and working to base, using values #3, #2 and #1 of your choice, with #1 yellow green at the base.

B. Closed herringbone in #3 green.

C. Double lazy daisy. First loop in value #1, second loop in value #2.

D. Long and short, with green values #2, #3 and #4 from outer edge to base.

Design Unit 127

Your own color selections.

A. Satin stitch in value #2.

B. Either seed stitch or closed herringbone, value #3.

C. Buttonhole stitch in value #4.

Design Unit 128

D. Laid work in #4 gold, tie with small seeds in #2 yellow green.

A. Long and short, beginning at top edge and working toward base, using #2 purple, #2 and #3 blue.

B. Repeat A, using #3 purple, #3 and #4 blue.

C. Chain, knot or outline stitches, working in direction of arrows, using #1, #2, #3, #4 and #5 blue, #5 purple.

E. Cretan stitch in #3 bright green.

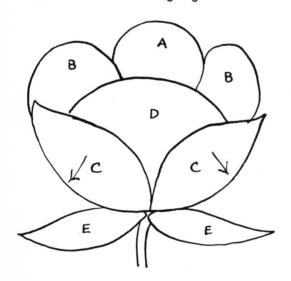

Design Unit 129

A. Satin stitch in #3 brick, then work over with small seed stitches in #2 bright yellow green.

B. Long and short in #1 and #2 brick. Couch over with #2 and #3 bright yellow green and tie with #4 brick.

C. Long and short in #4, #3, #2 and #1 rust.

D. Cretan stitches, using values in each leaf, as illustrated.

Design Unit 130

Some colors suggested, others of your choice.

A. Couch in #2 and #3 green, tie in #4 or #5 values of your choice.

B. Solid chain stitch, starting at top edge and working toward center, using #1, #2, #3, #4 and #5 values of your choice.

C. Long and short, starting at tip with #1 value of your choice, then working toward the base with #1, #2, #3 and #4 green.

D. Knot stitch in green, using #1 to #5 values, as shown.

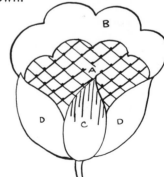

Design Unit 132

A. Cretan stitch in #1 green.

B. Satin stitch in #2 green.

C. Solid chain in rust, rose or brick, with value sequences as shown.

D. Satin stitch in color used in C, with value sequences as shown.

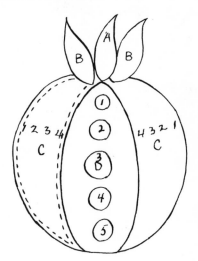

Design Unit 133

A. Cretan stitch in #1 green.

B. Cretan stitch in #2 green.

C. Couch in #3 and #4 rose, rust or brick, tie in #3 green.

D. Satin stitch in #3 value of color in C.

E. Satin stitch in #4 value of color in C.

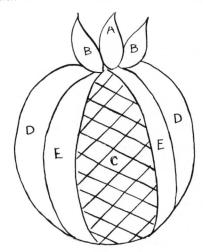

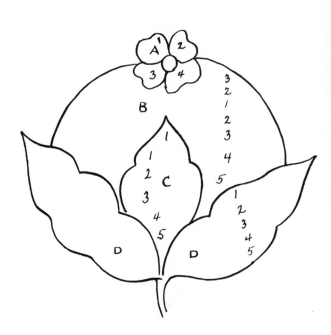

Design Unit 131

A. The small flower in satin stitches, with one value of pale green in each petal, as shown. French knot center in #3 gold.

B. Long and short in value sequences as indicated, using rust, rose or brick.

C. Long and short, starting at the tip with #1 value of the color used in B, then working toward the base, using #1 to #5 greens as shown.

D. Chain or knot stitch, using green values indicated.

DIVERS FLOWERS AND FRUIT

Courtesy Victoria & Albert Museum, Flowers in English Embroidery.

These traditional designs are among the most popular in all of crewel embroidery. They include the familiar thistle, symbolic of Scotland; the wheatear, golden emblem of bounty; the hollyhock spire, so well adapted to buttonhole stitches in combination with seeds or French knots; the strawberry, one of the oldest motifs and one of the most satisfying to make, and a few other examples with unusual pods, buds or petals.

The various shapes lend themselves to attractive groupings in designs featuring scattered motifs; in equally versatile fashion, they can be used separately.

They are all fairly easy to work, offer a choice of color and stitch possibilities and make attractive additions to almost any pattern.

Design Unit 134

Your own color selections.

A. Long and short, with value sequences as shown. Tipping the petal with an accent color is effective.

B. One row of outline stitches in #3 value of your choice.

C. Seed stitches in #3 of a contrasting color.

D. Solid chain in green, with value sequences as shown.

E. Cretan or Rumanian stitch in #4 green.

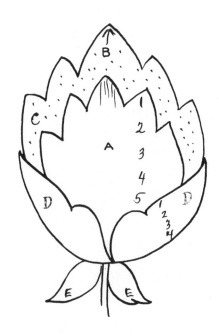

Design Unit 135

Your own color selections.

A. Long and short, in value sequences #3, #2 and #1.

B. Repeat, using #1, #2 and #3.

C. Repeat, using #2, #3 and #4.

D. One row of chain in #2 value.

E. Buttonhole in #3 value.

F. Seed stitch in #3 of a contrasting color.

G. Herringbone in #3 green, tie with #4 of a contrasting color. Edge petals in outline stitch, #4 green.

H. Tips in satin stitch, #3 gold; stems in outline stitch, #1 green.

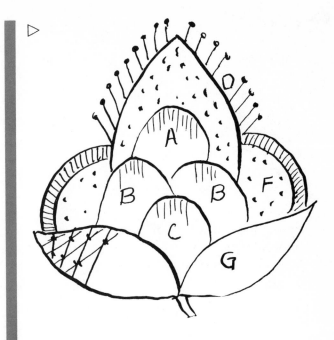

Design Unit 136

A. Satin stitches in gold values shown. Edge each small petal in #3 golden brown, using outline stitch.

B. Long and short, using brick value sequences as shown.

C. *Repeat B.*

D. French knots in #3 brick.

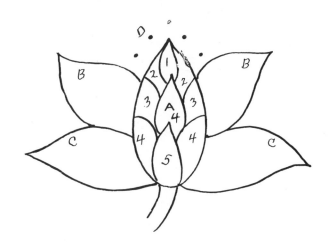

Design Unit 137

Directions basically the same as for Unit 138, using scattered French knots instead of seed stitches. Do the buttonhole or satin stitches in values indicated.

Design Unit 138

A. Knot stitch in #1 or #2 bright green.

B. Work the crescent-shaped portions of all petals (B through G) in satin or buttonhole stitches, using color of your selection in values below:

    B—#1
    C—#2
    D—#3
    E—#4
    F—#4
    G—#5

H. Seed lower portions of all petals in #2 or #3 bright green.

I. Long and short in green, with value sequences as indicated.

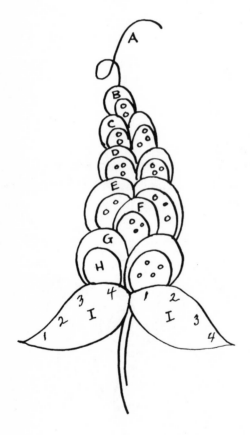

Design Unit 139

Work the crescent-shaped petals in either satin or buttonhole stitches, using color of your selection in values below:

    A—#5
    B—#4
    C—#3
    D—#2
    E—#1

F. Satin stitch in #1 green.

G. Entire stem worked in two rows of outline stitches, with #2 and #3 green.

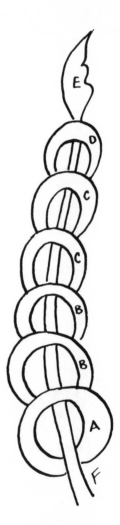

178

Design Unit 140

A. Laid work in #4 green. Couch in #3 and #4 purple, tie in #2 purple.

B. Long and short, in purple values as shown.

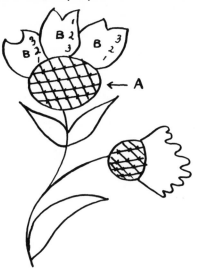

Design Unit 141

A. Outline stitch in #1 and #2 bright yellow green.

B. Satin or Cretan stitch in color of your selection, using value sequences shown.

C. Long and short. Tip scalloped edge with #1 gold, followed by #1 and #2 bright yellow green.

D. Repeat, using #2 gold with #3 and #4 bright yellow green.

Design Unit 142

Strawberries. Hulls of all three berries worked in Cretan or satin stitches, using #2 or #3 bright green, Stems in knot or outline stitches, using #3 or #4 bright green.

A. Laid work in strawberry, values #4 and #5. Scattered seeds in #1 bright yellow green.

B. Long and short, starting at the hull and working toward the tip, using strawberry, in values #5 and #4, brushing the tip with #3. Seeds in #1 bright yellow green.

C. Laid work in strawberry, values #4 or #5. Couch in #3 and #4 bright yellow green, tie with #1 bright yellow green.

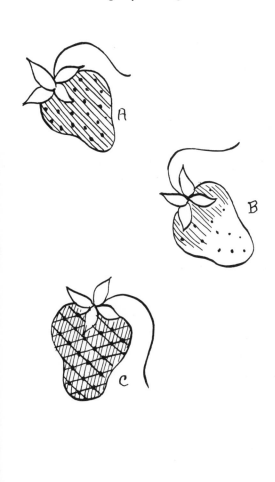

179

INSECTS

Odd winged insects were extravagantly used in old crewel pieces and are frequently worked into modern patterns with equal enthusiasm. They add color and interest to almost any design and can be subtly introduced into space-filler roles where patterns may need just a little more embroidery. They make wonderful color accent points, too.

Design Unit 143

Butterfly.

A. Top edge of wing in slightly opened button-hole stitches; other wing edge (F) in outline stitches; both in #2 gold. Scattered seeds in #3 olive green for remaining wing area.

B. Repeat, using #1 gold and #2 olive green.

C. Repeat, using #3 gold and #3 olive green.

D. Laid work in #4 olive green. Tie down with open chain in #4 gold.

E. Feet and antennae in outline stitch, #2 olive green; antennae tips in French knots, #3 gold.

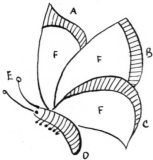

Design Unit 144

Moths. Colors of your own selection. Body in solid satin stitches, using values #4 or #5. Wings in solid long and short of lighter values, with sprinkling of seeds in contrasting color. Antennae in outline stitches, value #2.

 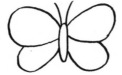

Design Unit 145

Bee.

Body in alternating black and gold satin stitches. Wings in small black outline stitches. Antennae and legs in tiny outline stitches.

Design Unit 146

Butterfly.

A. Buttonhole in #2 blue.

B. Repeat, using #3 blue.

C. Satin stitch in #3 khaki.

D. Repeat, using #1 gold.

E. Repeat, using #2 gold.

F. Seed in #3 purple.

G. Repeat, using #4 purple.

H. Outline stitch in #2 khaki. Tips in French knots, #3 gold.

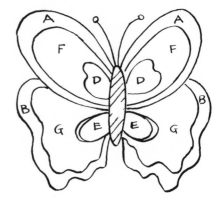

Design Unit 147

Butterfly.

A. Long and short in #1, #2 and #3 blue. Add three small satin dots in #3 rose.

B. Satin stitch in #3 rose, seed over in #5 green.

C. Long and short in #3 and #4 blue, seeded in #5 green.

D. Body in satin stitch, #4 khaki. Antennae in outline stitch, #2 khaki.

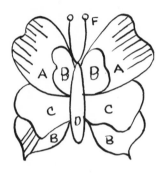

Design Unit 148

Butterfly.

A. Long and short in #1 and #2 purple.

B. Repeat, using #2 and #3 purple.

C. Edge with outline stitch in #3 purple; fill with satin stitches, #2 gold.

D. Repeat, using #4 purple and #3 gold.

E. Body in satin stitch, #4 green. Antennae in outline stitch, #1 green.

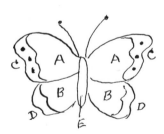

Design Unit 149

Butterflies.

A. Wings in long and short, starting at upper edges and working toward body, using #1 yellow green, #1 and #2 rose. Scatter seeds in #5 rose. Body in satin stitch, #4 golden brown; antennae in outline stitch, #2 brown.

B. Worked in colors of your own selection. Tip right wing in outline stitch, then fill with small satin dots in a contrasting color. Edge left wing in buttonhole stitch, then fill with small seeds in a contrasting color. Body in satin stitch; antennae in outline stitch.

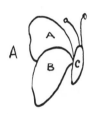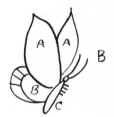

Design Unit 150

Butterfly.

A. Long and short in #4 and #3 rose, seeded in #2 bright yellow green.

B. Satin stitch in #1 bright yellow green.

C. Long and short in #1, #2 and #3 rose, with three small satin dots in #5 rose.

D. Body in satin stitch, using #5 and #4 olive green. Feet and antennae in outline stitch, #2 olive green; antennae tips in knot stitch, #4 rose.

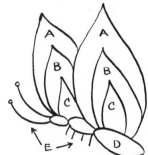

BIRDS AND ANIMALS

Embroiderers, ancient and modern, have always enjoyed embellishing their work with birds and animals—some realistic, some exotic and some mythical. Modern usage tends toward the realistic, although you are quite likely to find hares and deer of the same size nestled close by each other, without so much as a second thought as to whether one is as large, or as small, as the other. Such is the persuasive charm of crewel embroidery!

In addition to the several birds and animals shown here others are scattered throughout the book as small random decorations.

Design Unit 151

Deer.

Antlers: Small outline stitches worked solidly from tips to head, successively using #3 golden brown, #3 gold, #2 and #1 golden brown, #2 gold.

Ear: Satin stitch in #3 golden brown.

Head: Long and short in golden brown, value sequences as shown. Eye in satin stitch, #4 golden brown.

Tail: Long and short, using #1 and #2 golden brown.

Body: Long and short in golden browns, value sequences as shown.

Legs: Satin stitch in golden browns, value sequences as shown.

Accent the shadows with tiny outline stitches in #3 golden brown.

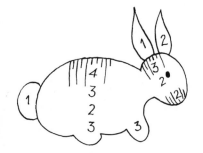

Design Unit 152

Rabbit or hare.

Grey or chocolate brown suggested.

Ears: Satin stitch, values as shown.

Body: Long and short, value sequences as shown.

Eye: French knot in value #5.

Tail: French knots in value #1.

182

Design Unit 153
Squirrel.
Grey suggested.
Tail: Long and short, with value sequences as shown.
Note stitch direction.
Body: Same as tail.
Legs: Solid outline stitch, with value sequences as indicated.
Ears: Satin stitch, values as shown.
Eye: French knot in value #5.

Design Unit 154
Owl.
Chocolate brown suggested.
A. Satin stitch in value #3.
B. Satin stitch in value #4.
Eye: Buttonhole in #2 gold, radiating around French knot centers in #2 brown.
Body: Buttonhole in browns, with value sequences as shown.
Talons: Two pairs of straight running stitches in #3 gold.

Design Unit 155
Bird.
Head: Buttonhole in #3 blue, radiating around the eye.
Eye: French knot in #5 blue.
Beak: Satin stitch in #3 gold.
Wing: Long and short. Tip scalloped edge in #1 gold, then work across, using #1, #2 and #3 blue in succession.
Body: Solid outline stitch. Begin with #1 gold, then use 5-value blue sequence as shown.
Tail: Satin stitch in gold or blue, using values #3, #2 and #1 as shown.

Design Unit 156
Bird.
Wings: Long and short. Tip in #1 aqua blue, then work chocolate brown in 3-value sequence as shown.
Comb: Satin stitch in #2 chocolate brown.
Head: Long and short, using #2 and #3 aqua blue.
Eye: French knot in #4 chocolate brown.
Body: Small buttonhole in gradations of chocolate brown as shown.
Tails: Satin stitch; center tail #2 aqua blue, other two #3 chocolate brown.
Legs and talons: Outline stitch in #5 chocolate brown.

CHAPTER SEVEN

DIVERS FLORA, FAUNA AND FANCIES:
a compendium of devices
associated with crewel embroidery motifs

This compendium, devoted largely to the folklore of the fauna, flora and fancies of crewel embroidery, is intended primarily as a diverting collection of words and phrases which may provide colorful footnotes to the history of this work. They may take you down odd and unexpected byways and some distance from the actual process of embroidery, but for the reader who enjoys quaint phrases as well as patterns, these comments may add still another dimension to the enjoyment of this art.

Such a compendium or glossary, spanning the centuries during which the heritage of crewel embroidery was built up stitch by stitch, naturally contains a few archaic words seldom encountered today, but there are other well-worn ones familiar to the ear and tripping on the tongue, whether they be diminutive names for garden or field flowers or salty, saucy expressions once very much a part of daily life. This list cannot be all-inclusive, since there is no single repository of all known examples of crewelwork to serve as a complete guide, but it is a representative one. An occasional isolated motif is included, such as the morris dancers, once a part of the pageantry of a "Merrie England," and incorporated in a unique example, the Abigail Pett curtain (page 28).

Some meanings associated with this art have remained relatively unchanged during several hundred years, but in many cases the original colorful associations have been lost. In this we are the poorer, for our forebears coined much that was—and is—picturesque in our language. For the pleasure of the modern reader, the meanings and associations these words enjoyed during the sixteenth, seventeenth and eighteenth centuries in England and colonial America are noted, with examples of the words in use.

A special word should be said about the difficulty of culling symbolic and emblematic associations from the past. To attempt specific interpretations of the varied elements prominent in the whole pageant of crewel embroidery is almost impossible. Not every carnation was a pledge of loyalty to Mary Stuart, nor every Tudor rose a renewal of fealty to Elizabeth Tudor. Many of these lovely flowers and their companions were created and embroidered simply for decorative appeal without any consideration of symbolic overtones. The reader is thus free to interpret, conjecture or weave romantic fantasies at will.

As for the animal kingdom—birds, beetles, butterflies and beasts large and small—many embroiderers may appreciate information about those well known to early embroiderers or associated with fable and folklore. A descriptive phrase or two may also be of help to those who might like to create a design with, for instance, an appropriate bird or a deer trippant.

For prosaic detail, the embroiderer may consult any number of helpful flower and bird books. For a change from assiduous attention to fine stitchery, perhaps this compendium will provide a rest for the fingers and a feast for the imagination—from cuckooflowers to unicorns.

Acanthus

The large, elegant leaves of this Mediterranean plant were much copied in classical architecture. It is famed as the leaf motif in the traditional leaf-and-scroll capital of the Corinthian column, said to be the most beautiful capital design ever created. One type has a spiny leaf, and another a broad, blunt leaf.

Acorn

After Charles Stuart spent one day hiding in an oak tree near Boscobel during his flight through England in 1651, this tree became known as "The Royal Oak" and this lowly nut took on a new significance. "Acornes were good till bread was found." (Bacon, 1597)

Anemone

The Greek root for the windflower, as it is known in England, means "daughter of the wind." Its lovely colors include white, yellow, several shades of purple and many kinds of red. "Anemone hath the name because the floure never openeth it self, but when the wind bloweth." (Turner, 1551)

Asparagus

This green vegetable, with its airy, ferny fronds, was known as "sperage," "'sparagus" and "sparrow-grass" in sixteenth- and seventeenth-century England until its name became formalized as "asparagus." "Sparrow-grass is so general that 'asparagus' has the air of stiffness and pedantry." (Walker, 1791) One Elizabethan writer reported the dark suspicion that it orginated from "Rammes hornes buried in the ground."

Bee

This industrious black-and-gold insect buzzes from flower to flower, setting a model of bustling activity as exemplified by the phrase "busy as a bee," which was familiar in the sixteenth century as well as "bees in the head," indicating a swarm of whims and fantasies. "The Bey is but a small beast amonge the foules, yet is her fruit exceadinge swete." (Cloverdale, 1535)

Beetle

The shell-like upper wings of this insect were observed to close over its back, thus protecting the true wings underneath. To be "blind as a beetle" was to be obtuse. "With such Betle arguments as you make." (Stapleton, 1566)

Bestiary

Many fanciful beasts found in embroidery designs were drawn from one or another of the allegorical treatises so popular during the Middle Ages. These books depicted animals of all sorts, some inhabiting the world of reality, others the world of imagination. The fabulous cockatrice, griffin, phoenix and unicorn, occasionally found in crewel embroideries, are to be found within the pages of a bestiary.

Bird of Paradise

When Magellan's ship touched New Guinea in 1522 two skins from these exotic birds were prepared by the natives for presentation to the king of Spain. The legs and thereupon feet were removed, a circumstance which gave rise to the European fable that these birds flew continuously, lived high in the sky far above man's vision and carried their eggs and young in a hollow on the males back. The magnificence of these birds was so overwhelming that they gained the name of visitors from paradise. The female and the young are plain, while the colors of the male span the rainbow in the most brilliant plumage in all creation. "The Bird of Wonder dyes, the Mayden Phoenix." (Shakespeare, *Henry VIII*)

Bluebell

This delicate bell-shaped blue flower, occasionally confused with the harebell, is the bonny bluebell of Scotland and the north of England. It is to be found in summer and fall in dry, open, rolling country. Elizabethan herbalists praised it.

Bluebottle

This is the common name for the blue cornflower, suggested by its resemblance to a leather bottle, although the term has been vaguely applied to other blue flowers. It was sometimes called "hurtsickle" because its hard, tough stem was a hazard to sickle blades. It was also a nickname for a minor public official wearing a dark blue uniform, a town crier or law-court officer. "I will have you as soundly swing'd for this, you blue-bottle." (Shakespeare, *Henry IV*)

Borage

This bright blue-flowered herb, its stems and leaves covered with prickly hairs, was used medicinally and as a salad and was also much esteemed as a cordial in England. The borage family includes the heliotrope and forget-me-not.

Butterfly

The varicolored, gossamer butterfly, with its delicate antennae and its scaled wings, has been regarded a symbol of frivolity and also of modesty. It is regarded as deeply symbolic in Oriental art. "And what's a Butterfly? At best He's but a caterpillar drest." (Gay, 1726) "All the butterfly men were at court last night." (Pendarves, 1728) "The butterflye glorieth not in her owne dedes." (Latimer, 1548)

Camel

The two types of this desert beast-of-burden—the one-humped Dromedary from Arabia (a lighter, faster variety) and the slower two-humped Bactrian variety—were known in England as early as the twelfth century when caravans from the East brought chests of wondrous spices and silks to Europeans.

Canterbury bells

These flowers have been called Coventry bells, Marian's violets, cuckoo flowers and ladie-smocks in various parts of England. Shakespeare described them as silver-white, but there is a touch of lilac in their petals. The name was associated in popular fancy with the little bells worn by the horses of pilgrims wending their way to Canterbury for prayers at the tomb-shrine of Thomas à Becket.

Cardinal

This bird, also called a cardinal finch, is known in America as a redbird. Its coat of feathers is a bright medley of reds, striking in its effect. Several other distinctive birds in this family include the blue grosbeak, painted bunting and spectacular pyrrhuloxia.

Carnation
See also *Pink*

This is the general name for cultivated varieties of the clove pink, clove gillyflower or gillyflower, as it was known in English gardens. It was originally spelled "coronation," which aptly suggests its early use in garlands, wreaths and crowns. It is also thought that its name may have originated from the word "carne" (flesh, i.e., flesh-colored). Carnations added a spicy flavor to ales and wines and were popularly called "sops in wine" by Elizabethan *bon vivants*. To many the carnation was a Stuart family emblem.

Caterpillar

In nature this fuzzy, sluggish object is the serpentine larva of a butterfly or moth; in English metaphor it was a symbol of a rapacious person, a plunderer, from the word "piller," "pillage," etc. ". . . cater-pillars of the common-wealth, hateful to all good people" (Weever, 1631). The caterpillar is also said to have been a Stuart emblem.

Chick

Many years ago chick was the singular of chicken, the common domestic fowl, as ox is the singular of oxen. Young chickens were called birds, "a henne and her byrdes."

Chinoiserie

This term refers to exotic Chinese motifs as Europeans imagined them in designs for fabrics, furniture and other aspects of interior decoration during the centuries when China was largely closed to foreigners.

The phrase was adopted from the French word "Chinois" for the Chinese, who were believed to be a fabulous people "living on the bounds of the earth." In a broad sense it suggested the Orient, or where the sun came up. "To be oriental is no other thing than to rise before the sun." (Lilly, 1647)

Cinquefoil

This term is applied to plants with five leaves or petals or leaves with five leaflets.

Cock, Cockerel

The cock, especially the game cock, was considered a most pugnacious, fearless bird. Cock-fighting was a favorite pastime of the Elizabethan sporting gentry and accounts for the phrase "cock o' the walk." When the cock's crow hailed the coming dawn all skulking denizens of darkness were expected to flee, leaving decent citizens to breathe easily once again until night settled upon the land.

Cockatrice

This member of the fanciful bestiary fold was a fearsome reptile, hatched by a serpent from a cock's egg, with the head, wings and feet of a cock set upon the body of a serpent with a barbed tail. The cockatrice was a medieval invention growing out of an even older mythological beast, the basilisk, which could slay by its odor, breath or look. "The cockatrice . . . which slay men by the poison of their sight." (Stubbes, 1583)

Columbine

This is an old-fashioned garden plant with a name derived from the Latin word for dove, "columba," thought to have been suggested by the flower's fancied resemblance to a cluster of doves. Parkinson (1629) described its colors as white, blue, violet, flesh color, pale and deep red, purple or mulberry. It was among the very first flowers to be brought to America by the colonists.

Convolvulus

This family, which includes the morning-glory, is noted for its graceful, slender, twining stems, its heart-shaped leaves and large white or purple-blue flowers.

Cony
See also *Hare, Rabbit*

Cornflower

This is a generic name given to various plants found growing in cornfields, although most often applied to the bluebottle. In America the cornflower is also known as the bachelor's button.

Cowslip

The common name for this down-to-earth member of the primrose family was derived from Anglo-Saxon words meaning cow-dung, probably in recognition of the flower's preference for cow-pastures. The oxlip is a relative. These fragrant yellow flowers were the "fairy cups" of popular folklore; Shakespeare's Ariel of *The Tempest* lay in a cowslip's bell.

Crowflowers

This seems to have been a popular name for the buttercup, but appears to have been applied to other flowers as well; "wild hyacinth or bluebell" (Tannahill); "Crow floures, Wilde Williams, Marsh Gilloflours and Cockow Gelofloures" (Gerard). Other names for them are crowfoot and king cup.

Cuckoo Bird

This well-known bird lays its eggs in other birds' nests, a characteristic noted by the Anglo-Saxons in their word for a betrayed husband, "cuckold." In flight, the cuckoo resembles the sparrow hawk, or kestrel. Its coloration is gray or white, with a gray throat and barred underbody. It is sometimes called the Hawk of May. "In May begynnis the golk to gaill (In May the cuckoo begins to sing)." (Scott, c. 1560)

Cuckoo Flower

This is a more or less random popular name given various wild flowers which are in bloom when the cuckoo bird is heard, occasionally applied to crowflowers, ladie-smocks, ragged robin, meadow pinks, etc.

Currant

This dried fruit of the dwarf seedless grape grown in the Levant and called "Corinth" after the city of that name was much esteemed for use in flavorings and preserves. Occasionally the name was mistakenly applied to gooseberries. "Redde Gooseberries; Bastard Corinthes." (Lyte, 1578)

Daffodil

This jaunty frilled yellow flower of the narcissus family is a welcome harbinger of spring in England and America. "Daffy-down-dilly" was a quaint term also associated with rustic maidenhood. "Many idle and ignorant gardeners do call some of these Daffodills Narcisses, when as all know that know any Latine, that Narcissus is the Latine name, and Daffodil the English of one and the same thing." (Parkinson, 1629)

Daisy

The English daisy's ray florets are of white or pink, with disk florets of a bright golden yellow. Its name derives from "day's eye," in reference to the flower's appearance and its habit of opening in the morning and closing at night. The American daisy is known as ox-eye in England.

Deer
See *Hind, Stag*

Dog

Many old folk sayings referred to canine habits: "hair of the dog that bit you," "old dog," "die like a dog," "wake a sleeping dog," "gone to the dogs," etc. and even Queen Elizabeth I used a common phrase, "Notwithstanding, as a dog hath a day, so may I perchance have time to declare (my intentions) in deeds."

Dove

Doves and pigeons are members of the same immediate family, but the term "pigeon" is usually applied to the larger, square-tailed of the species and "dove" to the smaller, more graceful members of the family. European and North American doves and pigeons are quietly clad, while those of tropical regions are quite colorful. The dove was possibly the first wild bird to be domesticated and, since the days of Noah and the Ark, has, along with the homing pigeon, traditionally provided man with an air-borne means of sending messages. The dove is an emblematic messenger of peace, symbolic of gentleness and guilelessness. It was also a word for an innocent, loving woman. In Christian symbolism it is the Holy Ghost or Dove of Heaven. "To pluck a pigeon" was to cheat a player in a game of chance.

Dragonfly

Next to the butterfly, this insect, with its iridescent body and wing colors that often glisten like jewels in the sunlight, is acknowledged as the most graceful and lovely of all the winged tribe, and by far the best acrobat.

Eagle

This bird, also called the bird of Jove, has been symbolic of majesty, authority and power in many countries for many centuries. Two species, the golden and the white-tailed, are native to England. The latter is similar to the American bald eagle. The eagle and the lion share the distinction of being regarded as the noblest and most regal of their respective species. This pre-eminence is merged in the body of the griffin, half-eagle, half-lion.

Elephant

The medieval bestiaries vied in awesome descriptions of this largest of four-footed mammals. One described the elephant as "having the form of a mountain, with a nose called a proboscis, which looks like a snake." Other features were noted in such quaint observations as these. "He has no joints in his knees, so if he falls he cannot rise. Hence he sleeps propped against a tree. The shrewd hunter partially saws through the elephant's favorite sleeping tree, so when he leans against it the tree topples over and the elephant falls to the ground. The Persians and Indians build wooden towers upon his back and fight each other with spears thrown from these castles. The elephant protects himself with his two ivory tusks [often pictured as growing straight up like those of a boar]. The elephant fears no other beast no matter how fierce, but he is frightened of a mouse."

Emblem
See also *Symbol*

A flower or animal was often adopted as a visible sign, of loyalty to a family, country or cause, etc.

Falcon

Falcons, considered symbols of fearless courage and power, were specially trained female hawks, taught to pursue other birds and small game, by keepers. Falconry was supposedly introduced into Europe from the Orient by returning Crusaders. The male hawks, called tercels, were considered less adaptable to training. The royal family used gerfalcons; earls, the peregrine; ladies, the merlin; yeomen, the goshawk; and servants, the kestrel, or sparrow hawk. Common hawks were considered merely rapacious.

Fern

In English folklore feathery ferns were possessed of magic powers, said to flower at twelve on Midsummer Night (June 21), although the blossoms were mysteriously picked before dawn by emissaries of Satan. If, by some stroke of fortune, anyone found a blossom before it was snatched up by a demon, one was immediately presumed vested with the power to become invisible, to perform daring deeds, consummate one's most ardent desires, to defy the Devil himself. "We steal as in a castle, cock-sure. We have the receipt of fern-seed, we walk invisible." (Shakespeare, *Henry IV*)

Finch

This bird family of Old World seed-eaters includes the familiar canary, the European goldfinch and the bullfinch. The canary and goldfinch are popular cage birds, pleasant songsters, easy to maintain. The goldfinch has a black-tipped white bill, scarlet forehead and upper throat, with the remainder of his head black, a cinnamon-brown back, broad black and yellow wing bands, black tail and a white underbody. The bullfinch has a black head, reddish breast and underbody, gray, black and white wings and a black tail.

Fleur-de-lis

This graceful three-part flower, also called fleur-de-lys and flower-de-luce, has long been an emblem of France and part of the French royal arms. As early as the sixteenth century these flowers of the iris plant were used to mark north on the compass and on maps.

Fly

This minute, ubiquitous winged insect's capacity for intrusion into even the most carefully guarded quarters early earned it equation with the powers of darkness. "A flie, otherwise called a divell." (Scot, 1548) The word was also a synonym for a flatterer, parasite or spy. The sixteenth century had fishing flies, and the seventeenth century had fly wheels and cosmetic flies, patches for the face. "(They) sent away your second messenger with a flie in his eare." It meant having received a severe rebuke, an adaptation from the earlier "flea in his ear." Flies were sometimes added to flower paintings and to crewel designs to provide spots of interest or color.

Fox

This fleet-footed animal, regarded as the personification of artful cunning, might have suffered the same fate as the wolf and wild boar (extinct in England before the sixteenth century) but for the sport his pursuit provided. The exhilarations of the fox hunt seemed to balance off the many transgressions of this wily red-brown quadruped—mischievous rascal, poacher, fowl-pen despoiler. "When the foxe preacheth, then beware of our geese," was a sixteenth-century saying.

Foxglove

This is a common ornamental flower whose botanical name, Digitalis purpurea, indicates its well-known medicinal value as a heart stimulant. Although the origin of the "fox" portion of its name remains obscure, it is obvious that the "glove" part stems from the finger-stall shape of the orchid, white and pink flowers, called "Iron-colour'd Fox-gloves" by Evelyn (1664).

Frog

This gentle green hoarse-voiced amphibian lent his name to a folk saying, "to have fished and caught a frog," which signified a disappointing ending to an ambitious project. "The croaking of frogs is well

known, and from that in fenny countries they are styled Dutch nightingales or Boston Waites." (Pennant, 1769). "Waits" were the groups of wind instrumentalists maintained by cities and towns to play upon ceremonial occasions, such as when welcoming her Majesty Queen Elizabeth on her various royal progresses.

Gillyflower

This was the common name given flowers which had a clove-like scent—various types of pink, the wall-flower, occasionally the carnation. It might be spelled gilly- or gilli, ending with -flowers, -floures, -flores or -fers. "The Julyflower, as they are most properly called (though vulgurly Gillyflower and Gillofer)." (Holme, 1688)

Gooseberry
See Currant

Grape

Along with the fig and the pomegranate, the grape is "as old as man." The grape is thought to have originated many centuries ago in Asia Minor, as early mosaics showing details of grape culture and wine-making have revealed, and spread from there to Greece, Sicily and France, and to England by means of the Romans. Grapes are raised for wine, for the table, for raisins and for sweet juices. By the sixteenth century in England the bottled and fermented grape had given birth to such proverbial observations as "When the wine is in, the wit is out" (Draxe, 1616); "You praise the wine before you taste of the grape" (Heywood, 1546); and "Good wine needs no bush," which was a reference to the vintner's sign, the ivy bush, or vine.

Grasshopper

"This insect bee so well knowne it needeth no other description" might be a comment applied to this familiar resident of midsummer fields and a character in the old fable of the grasshopper and the ant. During the sixteenth century there were two attitudes concerning the spry green creature: "They be blessed & happy that wyll apply & dispose themselfe with the greshopper to lepe up as hye as they may" (Pilgr. Perf. W. de. W, 1526) and "Such pleasaunce makes the Grashopper so poore" (Spenser, 1579).

Griffin

This fabulous beast with the head and wings of an eagle and the body and hind-quarters of a lion dates back many centuries, as attested by old Greek coins bearing its image. The griffin was a fierce-looking creature and reputedly extremely vigilant, especially in guarding treasure. The griffin, being a compound of two of the noblest of beasts, was adopted into the heraldic arms of many European noble families.

Hare

This furry quadruped, with its long quivering ears and fleet hind legs, was much mentioned in metaphor and proverb: "to hold with the hare and run with the hounds," which was to play a double game, to be deceitful; "to have two hares afoot," which was to have too many irons in the fire; "to catch a hare with a drum," which was to attempt the impossible; "to get the hare's foot to lick," which was to receive small reward for one's efforts; and "to make hare ·of," which was to ridicule. Hares were considered by some to be bad omens and thought to be associated with witches; if a hare were to cross a man's path he would be wise to retrace his steps immediately. Medieval belief held hares to be melancholy animals and capable of passing on this affliction to anyone who ate of their flesh.

Harebell

This name was used to denote the wild hyacinth, a blue flower common throughout England, sometimes mistakenly identified as the bluebell. "Our English Iacinth or Hare-bel is so common every where that it scarce needeth any description." (Parkinson, 1620). Parkinson listed the prevalent colors as a deep blue running toward purple or purplish red, various shades of a lighter blue, particolored blue and white and pure white.

Hart
See *Stag*

Hawk
See *Falcon*

Hamlet observed that he knew "a hawk from a handsaw," but most authorities believe Shakespeare intended the differentiation to be between a hawk and a heronshaw (heron).

Hawthorn

This thorny shrub or small tree has been extensively planted as a hedge. It is known for its white, red or pink blossoms and its dark berry, or "haw." The wood is extremely hard. "Before finding out the Needle our Fore-fathers are said to have made use of an Hay-thorn, or a Thorn Prick." (Holme, 1688)

Heartsease

In the sixteenth century this name was applied both to the pansy and to the wallflower. Later it was restricted to the latter. "The yellow Gillofer is called . . . Wall floures and Hartes ease." (Lyte, 1578)

Herbal

This term refers to a kind of book especially popular in Elizabethan England which classified, described and often illustrated plants, with specific reference to their medicinal properties. Early herbalists often strayed from their specialty into the field of general botany. Gerard's *Herbal* (1597) is often quoted.

Hind

This was the name given the female of the deer, especially the red deer, during and after its third year. "A milk-white Hind, immortal and unchang'd, Fed on the lawns." (Dryden, 1687)

Honeysuckle
See also *Woodbine*

This was the common name of the woodbine, a popular climbing shrub or vine, with fragrant, trumpet-shaped flowers in various colors. When applied to a person it was a term of praise and affection. "Who would not thinke him perfect curtesie? Or the honney-suckle of humilitie?" (Gilpin, 1598)

Hoopoe
See also *Nightingale*

This bird, a migratory visitor to England, was originally called a "hoop," perhaps in reference to its unusual crest, later a "hoop-hoop" in imitation of its repeated cry and finally a "hoopoe." This bird family was known to the ancient Egyptians. The hoopoe's crest, head, neck, breast and lower underbody are an orange-tinted light brown, its wings and tail a darker brown, with prominent white bands. The most striking feature is its high crest, which bears an amazing resemblance to the full headdress of an American Indian, tipped feathers and all.

Hummingbird

These tiny, exquisitely beautiful birds, known throughout the Americas from Alaska to Tierra del Fuego, are literally "avian jewels." Hummingbird skins were actually once fashioned into pins, brooches and other pieces of jewelry for feminine ornamentation.

Iris
See also *Fleur-de-lis*

This plant is known for its distinctive sword-shaped foliage and graceful flowers with three upright petals and three drooping sepals. In Greek mythology Iris was the messenger of the gods, and the rainbow served as her bridge from heaven to earth. The iris became the beloved fleur-de-lis emblem of France. The violet-scented root of this flower, orris, has been used medicinally, for flavoring and particularly in perfumes, powders and sachets. "Iris is knowen both of the Grecianes and Latines by that name; it is called in Englishe the flour de lyce." (Turner, 1562)

Jacobean

Although the term is generally applied to furniture, architecture, a prevailing style of decoration, and statesmen and writers of the reign of James I (Jacobus Britanniae Rex) (1603-1625) it has become a "convenience term" frequently used to denote the crewel embroideries created in the exotic idiom during the early seventeenth century.

Jay

This noisy, boldly aggressive bird, Cyanocitta cristata, is another bird that "needeth no description," for he generally makes his presence known. In America it is also known as a blue jay. Its English cousin's proper name is Garrulus glandarius. Its coloring is cinnamon and white with black and white accents and just a touch of blue in the wing bars. Not unexpectedly, the word "jay" as applied to a person meant an impertinent chatterer even as long ago as the fifteenth century.

Kingfisher

This is the name of a small bird of brilliant red and green plumage which feeds on fish which it has caught by diving. It is sometimes mistakenly called the halcyon, a legendary bird from the days of ancient Greece, fabled as making its nest upon the open seas during the winter solstice. By ancient belief the bird has a calming effect upon the waters from whence comes the expression "halcyon days."

Lamb

The gentle lamb has often been used as a religious symbol, the Lamb as the Son of God, and it has also been regarded as emblematic of sincerity. "It is comely for a man to be a lambe in the house, and a lyon in the field." (Puttenham, 1589). The word acquired a somewhat sinister cast, however, during the late seventeenth century because of the rapacious behavior of a certain Colonel Kirke's regiment during the rebellion against James II. The regimental flag displayed the Paschal Lamb; hence the bitterly ironical expression "Kirke's Lambs."

Lark

This European bird, dressed in unpretentious brown and gray, has been a "blithe spirit" for poets and an early-morning songster for poets and peasants alike. "Goe to bed with the Lambe, and rise with the Larke." (Lyly, 1580) From its ability to fly high came a proverbial expression, "When the Sky falls, we shall catch Larks," (1711) and a term, "skylark," meaning to cavort, or indulge in high jinks. The bird's exceptionally long-clawed rear toe is commemorated in a flower name: larkspur.

Leopard

The name for this animal comes from leo (lion) plus pard (the archaic name for panther), a combination illuminating an ancient fable that had not been wholly discredited as late as 1635. "There is no Leopard, or Libbard but such as is begotten between the Lion and the Panther." (Swan). The scientific name of this jungle cat also acknowledges the fable: Felis pardus. The proverb about the leopard changing its spots is an old one.

Lily

The lily is one of the oldest flowers known to man and has long been associated symbolically with his deepest experiences of life, death, and beliefs in or aspirations to immortality. It was also known as Juno's flower, its white color symbolic of the drops of milk spilled from the goddess's breast as she nursed the infant Hercules. The large varicolored flowers range in color from a serene white through many variations of red and purple, often marked by dark spots within the petals. Lilies were among the most important flowers in English gardens. "The Lilies oft obtaine Greatest sway, unless a blushe Helpe the Roses at a push." (Wither, 1622). They were also emblems of purity. "A Virgin, A most unspotted Lily." (Shakespeare, *Henry VIII*)

Lion

This majestic maned animal has long enjoyed a regal title as "King of Beasts." Since the time of James I (1603) a figure of a lion has been employed as the dexter supporter of the British royal arms, the sinister supporter being the Scottish unicorn. The folk saying that "March may roar in like a lion and depart like a lamb" is one which goes back at least as far as the seventeenth century. The "Lion of Cotswold" and the "Lion of Essex" (or Rumford) were ironical references to sheep and calves respectively.

Marigold

The golden, bright yellow or orange flowers of this plant of the genus Calendula (from calendar, recognizing the many months this lovely flower is in bloom) close every night and open dewy-eyed to the rising sun. "Canopied in darkness sweetly lay, Till they might open to adorn the day." (Shakespeare, *Lucrece*) They have also been called yellow-Goldes, Souvenirs, Mary-buds and Marygoldes. This flower lent itself to use in colorings, flavorings and medicines, especially marygold conserve, that "cureth the trembling of the harte."

Monkey

In the sixteenth century the words "monkey" and "ape" were sometimes used interchangeably. Monkeys are occasionally found in crewel embroideries, usually as part of chinoiserie designs. "A guilty conscience is as afraid of a feather as a monkey's tail of a whip" was a seventeenth-century proverb.

Morris Dance

This popular folk dance was introduced to England about 1500. The name derives from the Spanish Moors, or Moriscoes. Originally danced by five men and a boy dressed as Maid Marian, it later became associated with May Day and other festive holidays and its *dramatis personae* was expanded to include Robin Hood, Friar Tuck and Little John. Costumes of the dancers were ornamented with little bells tuned to sound in harmony. Banned by the Puritans under the Commonwealth, it thereafter faded into obscurity.

Moth

This small winged nocturnal insect is known for its fatal fondness for light. Housewives have long sought to keep them away from their cupboards and closets. "The Asshes of hym is gode to make white teth & to kepe the motes out of clothes." (Andrew, 1520)

Nightingale

'Tis the male of this celebrated member of the thrush family which is noted for its song. The melancholy, romantic bird of the poets has a reddish-brown back and a dull grayish-white underbody. Although it sings by day, its song in the stillness of moonlight is especially appealing to all who hear its philomelian airs. According to an old myth the nightingale was originally a tragic princess. Tereus, king of Thrace, married Procne, daughter of Pandion, king of Attica.

After their son Itys was born Tereus tired of Procne, desiring her sister Philomela instead. He sent Procne away, declaring her to be dead. His feigned bereavement so touched Philomela that she consented to take her sister's place at his side. When she discovered the truth her tongue was cut out and she was put into solitary confinement during which she spent the long hours weaving her tragic story into a robe, which she smuggled out to Procne. The sisters thereupon plotted their revenge: they planned to serve a dead Itys as food to his father. This they did and then fled, with Tereus in raging pursuit. Just before he overtook them the gods answered their prayers for deliverance and changed them all into birds. Philomela became a nightingale; Procne, a swallow; Tereus, a hoopoe. Itys was returned to life as a pheasant, and Pandion, who had died of grief at his daughter's dishonor, was restored to life as an osprey, Pandion haliaetus, closely related to the falcon.

Nut

Various domestic nuts and berries including acorns are occasionally shown in crewel embroidery. The word could mean things of small value, "But the nut is not worth cracking." (Fuller, 1655) A sixteenth-century proverb was "She is lost with an apple and won with a nut." It also meant a difficult problem. "Nowe knacke me that nut, maister Candidus." (Elyot, 1545). It also denoted pleasure. ". . . and such are Nuts to me." (Fletcher, 1617)

Oak

The mighty oak is intertwined with the history of Britain, going back to the time of the ancient Druids, who were said to have held their religious rites in oak groves at a time when vast areas of Britain were covered by oak forests. Many oaks are famous in English history—Abbot's Oak, the Major Oak in Sherwood Forest, Robin Hood's Larder (the hollow tree where, according to legend, Robin Hood hid his deer),

William the Conqueror's Oak, Parliament Oak, etc. Royal Oak Day, decreed by Parliament in 1664, commemorated Charles II's restoration to the throne. An oak had sheltered this royal fugitive near Boscobel, and acorns and oak leaves became traditional Stuart emblems. For a thousand years oak timbers were a part of sailing ships, and it is universally emblematic of stout hearts. The Charter Oak is a famous American tree.

Oriole

The name of this colorful bird comes from the Latin *aureolus,* meaning golden. The golden oriole is a migratory visitor to England, the only European member of the oriole family, which is largely near-tropical in origin. It is golden yellow except for black wings and tail, highlighted by glimpses of yellow. The most famed American oriole is the Baltimore oriole, so named because his orange and black plumage matched the colors in the coat of arms of Lord Baltimore of the Calvert family, colonial proprietors of Maryland.

Owl

This nocturnal bird of prey was considered to be solemn and dull in sixteenth-century England, not especially esteemed for its wisdom. "To fly with the owles" was to be a creature who kept late hours. The simian-like features of the familiar barn owl led it to be named "monkey-face." Other American owls are the barred, great horned, screech, pigmy and elf owls.

Padula

This word for small imaginative flowers grew up among workers in a craft indigenous to America.

Palampores, Palimpores

This was the name of a type of figured chintz material, usually polychrome, imported from India during the seventeenth century. "Staple Commodities are Calicuts white and painted, Palampores, Carpets, Tea." (Fryer, 1698)

Pansy

The pansy is the common name for the plant Viola tricolor, whose velvety, multicolored flower-faces were described by Gerard (1597) as ". . . of three sundry colours, whereof it took the surname Tricolour . . . purple, yellow, white or blewe." The wild pansy is a common weed often found in cornfields. The name is fancifully derived from the French pensée (thought).

"In English Hartsease, and Pansies of the French name *Pensées.* Some give it foolish names, Call-me-to-you and Three-faces-in-a-hood." (Parkinson, 1629). Other affectionate names for this modest flower include Johnny-Jump-Up, Love-in-Idleness, Pink-of-my-John, Fancy Flamey, and Kiss-me-at-the-Garden-Gate.

Panther

This animal was believed to be a large fierce cat of India with a black coat, or a tan or yellowish one with black spots. It is a colloquial name for medium-sized cats of the leopard family, sometimes applied to the mountain lion (puma) of North America, to the jaguar of Central and South America and to various leopards of India and Africa. A bestiary description of a panther included such qualities as a beautiful coating of several colors, an allspice-sweet breath and a disposition of such extraordinary kindness it regarded only a dragon as an enemy. "Panther, a kinde of spotted beast, the Leopard, or Libard being the Male, the Panther the Female." (Phillips, 1658)

Parrot

This brilliantly colored, talkative bird is a part of a large group which includes parakeets, cockatoos, macaws, lovebirds, budgerigars and others. The ancient Greeks and Romans noted the parrot's capacity for imitating human speech. They were popular birds as pets and often lived to ripe old ages in their cages. "Have you founde your tongue now, pretie peate? Then wee must have an Almon for Parratt." (Rich, 1581) "Children, like Parratts, soone learne forraigne languages, and sooner forget the same." (Moryson, 1617)

194

Peacock

The plumage of this gorgeous male, with his tail like a multi-jeweled fan, is indeed a challenge to the embroiderer's skill. A native of India, the peacock has become a symbol of pride and envy. The expressions "proud as a peacock" and "play the peacock" were well established in the vernacular of the seventeenth century. It has also been used as a religious symbol to indicate the Resurrection because of the annual renewal of the bird's gorgeous plumage after each moulting. In the classical legend Argus of the Hundred Eyes was changed into a peacock by an angry Juno, and his eyes formed the beautifully colored disks of the peacock's tail. Its awkward gait and harsh, strident cry have also caused this bird of Juno to be described as "slinking like a thief, with the voice of the devil and the garb of an angel."

Peapod

The pod or legume of the pea plant was known in the sixteenth and seventeenth century as a peascod, and a playfully dire imprecation of the day was "A peascod on you!"

Pelican

The white pelican is native to southeastern Europe, and the brown pelican to the American South. Its unusually capacious bill is an efficiently operated dip-net used by the pelican to supply his daily fish ration. A legend arose in the Middle Ages that the pelican fed its young on blood obtained by pecking its breast. "That blood already, like the Pellican, Thou hast tapt out, and drunkenly carowsed." (Shakespeare, *Richard II*)

Pennon

A pennon was an earlier name for the triangular or swallow-tailed flag or banner today called a pennant.

Peony

This plant, which was much used in sixteenth- and seventeenth-century "physick," derived its name from Paeon, as Apollo was sometimes known in his role as physician to the gods. The large, globular flowers have a color range of many pleasing shades of red, rose and white. "Peony the female groweth in every countrey, but I never saw the male saving only in Antwerp." (Turner, 1548)

Pheasant

The true pheasant is a bird of brilliant plumage rivaled only by birds of paradise and hummingbirds in the splendor of its coloring. Pheasants are mainly native to the Orient, and some Chinoiserie designs in crewel embroidery show these striking birds. The ring-necked game bird known as a pheasant in England and America was introduced to England by the Romans and brought to America in the late eighteenth century. "A Kinde of fowles which are commonly called Pheisants, but whether they be pheysants or not, I will not take upon me to determine." (Morton, 1637). English game laws of 1697 stated, "None shall take Fesants or Partridges with Engins."

Phoenix

This fabulous bird, a creation of Egyptian mythology, was regarded as sacred in the Land of the Nile. After a life span of several hundreds of years it was reputed to build a nest for itself of spice twigs, settle into it and thereupon be consumed in flames ignited by the sun and fanned by its own wings. From the ashes another phoenix would rise and the life cycle would begin all over again. This may have been one of man's earliest expressions of immortality. The word was also used to describe a paragon, someone of rare excellence. Queen Elizabeth I was so eulogized at her death in 1603. "Her late sacred Majestie, the rare Phoenix of her sex, who now resteth in glorie." (Knolles). The Chinese phoenix, often mentioned in descriptions of crewel embroidery, is described as "having the head of a pheasant, a cock's comb, the beak of a swallow, the neck of a tortoise and gorgeous plumage." It was considered a most benevolent creature, never stepping on plants nor pecking any living thing. The other three "fabulous animals of China" were the dragon, the unicorn and the tortoise.

Pink

These spicy flowers were favorites of English gardeners. "Called . . . by divers names, as Pynkes, Soppes in wine, feathered Gillofers, and small Honesties." (Lyte, 1578). They were also variously called Sweet Johns, Sweet Williams, London Pride (a speckled variety). Sweet Williams were among the first flowers to be brought to America by early colonists from English gardens. The original crimson and white shadings were vastly expanded into many allied colorings. A complimentary expression containing the phrase "pink" was "the pink of courtesy." "Pink" also meant an exquisitely lovely person, the embodiment of perfection. "He hath a pretty pinke to his own wedded wife." (Breton, 1602)

Pintadoes
See also *Palampores*

This was a popular name for a type of Oriental or chintz cloth painted or printed in colors. The word was taken from the Spanish and Portuguese *pintado,* meaning "painted." In the eighteenth century pintado also was the name for the pearled hen, known today as the common guinea fowl.

Pomegranate

This ancient and exotic fruit has long occupied a place of importance throughout the Orient alongside the fig and the grape. Associated in classical mythology with Persephone, an da symbol of fecundity, it was also celebrated as the fateful apple of the Garden of Eden. Considered indigenous to Persia and neighboring countries, it was said to have been a favorite fruit of Mohammed, who counseled, "Eat the pomegranate, for it purges the system of envy and hatred." It was known in England as early as 1300, and was some-times called a "Punic Apple." Its many seeds are enveloped in a juicy reddish pulp covered by a leathery rind of a rose or golden orange hue. Its flowers may be scarlet, or occasionally white or shades of yellow.

Potato

This plant, one of the convolvuli, was a novelty to sixteenth-century Europe. Potato flowers were incorporated in some crewel embroidery designs. It is believed to have been introduced into Spain from the West Indies about 1500. "In Hispaniola they dygge also certeyne rootes growynge of theim selves, which they caule Botatas . . . have the taste of rawe chestnuttes, but are sumwhat sweeter." (Eden, 1555) Credit for bringing the potato to Europe has been claimed for many, including Walter Raleigh and Francis Drake, to whom the Germans erected a monument in gratitude. Gerard carried the first authentic European account of the potato in his *Herbal* (1597), including an accurate woodcut of the plant. Even he erred, however, in calling it "Potato of Virginia," for the potato did not reach Virginia until well into the following century. It became tremendously popular throughout Europe. "Let the skie raine Potatoes." (Shakespeare, *Merry Wives of Windsor*)

Primrose

This flower has long been a prime favorite in English gardens. Its name comes from *prima rosa,* the first rose of the newly-awakening countryside. It is a cousin of the cowslip and oxlip. Harbinger of countless springs, its pastel tones are gently shadowed by luminous greens. Almost all imaginable color combinations of primrose now greet the spring, but true to ancient tradition the shades are never to be confused with the brighter shades of midsummer flowers.

Primula

This was a random name—"the firstling of spring"—applied to the primrose, cowslip, oxlip and field daisy, each of which was variously thought to be the first flower of spring.

Quatrefoil

This term is applied to plants with four leaves or petals or leaves with four leaflets.

Rabbit

The term "rabbit" was originally applied to the young hare, while the name for the adult animal was "cony." The English lop-eared breed had ears measuring approximately 10 inches long by 6 inches wide. "Rabbit" was a contemptuous term for a weak man but one of affection or innocence in the case of a woman or girl: "none so sweete as thy selfe, sweete conye moppe" and "my cloyster-bred conney." "Bunny" was a term of endearment for women and children in the late seventeenth century.

Robin

This popular member of the thrush family is cheerful, friendly and an excellent songster. While the American robin has back and wings of brown tinged with greenish olive and breast and underbody of deep red-orange, the smaller English robin, also known as a redbreast, has similar back and wing coloring, with a lighter red-orange breast and grayish-white lower underbody. In fable, English robins charitably covered the eyes of all dead creatures in the forest: "Covering with Mosse the dead's unclosed eye, the little Red-brest teacheth Charitie." (Drayton, 1604)

Rose

Called "the regent of them all" (Cowper, 1781), this flower has been a symbol of matchless perfection. It was a favorite when Rome and Athens were young, the flower which "by any other name" would be as sweet, the first flower of poets, playwrights, the high and mighty, the lowly and meek. It was considered the fairest in crewel gardens and has been used in medicine, perfumes, flavorings and confections. It has also been regarded as a symbol of beauty and silence.

Rose, Tudor°

During the War of the Roses the House of York adopted the white rose as its emblem, while the House of Lancaster traditionally took the red. When the strife was ended in 1485 with the accession of Henry VII (the first Tudor) he underscored his claim to the throne by the emblematic Tudor rose, which was a combination of the red and the white. This open-faced flower is sometimes shown with alternating red and white quarter-sections and sometimes as a white rose centered upon a slightly larger red rose.

Serpent, Snake

The terms "serpent" and "snake" are generally synonymous, although "serpent" suggests the larger venomous species. In symbolism the serpent was equated with Satan himself, the triumphant Tempter of frail man in the Garden of Eden. The snake was regarded as emblematic of human evils: malice, envy, jealousy, treachery and venomous gossip.

Sheep

A "wolfe in Sheepes array" (Shakespeare, *Henry VI*) was only a figure of speech, but a sheep in sheep's array was vital to the English economy. The wool industry apparently got its start in the British Isles about the time of the Roman conquest. By the Middle Ages English wools had attained a reputation for excellence. This fleecy, blunt-nosed quadruped was a byword for such characteristics as foolishness, timidity, bewilderment and defenselessness.

° Note: According to one authority (Christopher Morris, *The Tudors*, Macmillan, 1955) Henry VII may have deliberately promoted the myth of the Tudor double rose, symbolizing the healing of the rift, and the red rose of Lancaster may have been a "fabrication born of Henry VII's love for symmetry and symbols."

Snail

This small, slow, innocuous creature has long shared with the tortoise a reputation for exceedingly deliberate peregrinations. A native of East Africa, then transported to Madagascar and spreading to the Indo-Pacific area, this unusual little mollusc makes a pleasing decorative device. In an earlier time people "were wont to have paynted snayles in their houses." (Northbrooke, 1579)

Snowdrop

This plant, with its pendant white flowers, is one of the earliest of spring arrivals. "These purely White Flowers that appear about the end of Winter, and are commonly call'd Snow drops." (Boyle, 1664)

Squirrel

The name of this arboreal rodent comes from the Greek meaning "a shadow with a tail." The red squirrel has long been familiar in English woods, while the gray squirrel is an American native. The association of "squirrel brains" with flighty conduct is not new. "Having nothing but a few squirrils brains to help them frisk from one ill-favour'd fashion to another." (Ward, 1647)

Stag

This term refers to the male deer, especially the European red deer, during its fourth year. A one-year-old was a "calf." It was a "great stag" during its fifth year and a "hart" during its sixth and beyond. The ancients believed the stag could draw a serpent from its hole by its breath and crush it to death. Thus the stag as a destroyer of evil became associated with the Deity in Christian symbolism. At the vernacular level about 1600, to "go stag" was to be naked, to "wear a stag's crest" was to be made a cuckold and to "turn stag" was to be an informer.

Stork

The brilliant white plumage of this bird, a summer visitor to Europe, contrasts with its long red legs. Its virtues have been much praised. "Constancy is like unto a Storke who wheresoever she flye cometh into no nest but her owne." (Lyly, 1580) "He is a stork to his parent, and feeds him in his old age." (Fuller, 1642) The German-Dutch legend about the stork as a bringer of babies had made its way to England before 1600.

Strawberry

This rosy, luscious fruit was a favorite delicacy. "Voluntary strawberries are not so good as those that are manured in the gardens." (Venner, 1620) Izaak Walton saw a connection between his favorite sport and strawberries: "We may say of Angling as Dr. Boteler said of Strawberries: Doubtless God could have made a better berry, but doubtless God never did." The pulpit exhortations of "strawberry preachers" were annual events. ". . . bee so daintie as they are, which come from some Strawberrewise, that is, once a yeere." (Gardiner, 1606)

Sunflower

Although sunflower generally refers to a tall American plant with coarse foliage and conspicuous yellow flowers, the term has also been used for any flower that turns to follow the sun. The marigold was once termed a sunflower.

Swallow

This bird family, which includes the martins, covers nearly the whole globe, except for the two polar regions. This harbinger of spring is known simply as the "swallow" in England, the equivalent of "chimney swallow" in France and Germany, and the "barn swallow" or its equivalent in the United States, Holland and Norway. The proverb "One swallow does not a summer make" goes back at least to the sixteenth century.

Symbol

The word "symbol," which is generally synonymous with "emblem," is more often reserved for subjects of deeper significance, such as sacred beliefs.

Thistle

This plant, with its bristly purple flower heads, is the heraldic emblem of Scotland. It received its accolade as the "guardian thistle" during a fateful night attack upon Stirling Castle in the eighth century when the attacking Danes stepped barefooted upon thistles growing around the castle and sounded an alarm with their cries of pain. The name "thistle" has often been applied to any prickly plant, even the artichoke.

Thrush

This bird is a member of a large family which includes many notable songbirds—nightingales, song thrushes, wood thrushes, robins, bluebirds, hermit thrushes, solitaires, chats and wheatears. Two well-known English species are the song thrush, or throstle, and the missel thrush, fond of mistletoe berries and sometimes called storm cock since even squally weather did not still its song. Well-known North American species include the wood and hermit thrushes, the solitaire, bluebird and veery.

Tree of Life

The relation of the tree to man's life is unique; it has become inseparable from his needs. It has given him food, shelter, warmth, security against the ele-

ments, a resting-place for his departed, a means of travel upon the waters, a retreat from the scourges of his assailants, the material for arms to fashion against his enemies, a home for his gods and lesser spirits, a place of peace and quiet for meditation and a repository for his faith in immortality as each year the tree itself is renewed.

The Tree of Life concept appeared in numerous designs, particularly during the period when the exotic arboreal idiom was most prevalent. It has an affinity with Eastern designs. Moreover, the long-awaited King James Version of the Bible was published in 1611, and the imagery of its verses may have had some impact on the universal popularity of this motif. England was essentially a forested land and trees, or portions of trees, were already an accepted motif in embroidery. It is at least open to conjecture that the great variety of fruits, flowers, leaves and other extravagant ornamentation heaped upon the tree designs may have been inspired by the Old Testament tree of knowledge of good and evil or the Apocalypsean tree of life, with its twelve manner of fruits. "And out of the ground made the Lord God to grow every tree that is pleasant to the sight, and good for food; the tree of life also in the midst of the garden, and the tree of knowledge of good and evil." (Genesis 2:9) "In the midst of the street of it, and on either side of the river, was there the tree of life, which bare twelve manner of fruits, and yielded her fruit every month: and the leaves of the tree were for the healing of nations." (Revelation 22:2).

Trefoil

This term has been applied to any three-leaved plant such as clover, with leaves divided into three leaflets. Trafles is another old word for these.

Trippant

This is an old word for the position of a deer, or a member of a related family, with its right foot lifted and the other three placed on the ground as if trotting.

Tulip

The name for this flower comes from the Turkish pronunciation of the Persian word for turban, a head-covering which the tulip flower was thought to resemble. From Turkey the flower was introduced into Europe in 1554. In 1597, after about twenty years in England, Gerard described it in his *Herbal* as "Tulipa, or the Dalmatian cap . . . a strang and forreine floure." It remained a foreign flower outside the garden for some years before it became the center of a fever of speculation. "Such Fellow-commoners who come to the Univeristy only to see it and to be seen (are) call'd The University-Tulips, that make Gaudy shew for a while." (Mede, 1672)

Turkey

This bird was discovered by the Spanish in Mexico about 1518 and introduced into European larders by them. So fast did this bird spread throughout the continent that it soon became a traditional part of the delicacies prepared for a holiday feast. "Christmas fare . . . shred pies and turkey well drest." (Tusser, 1573)

Unicorn

This ancient legendary beast has the head and body of a horse, the hind legs of an antelope, the tail of a lion (sometimes that of a horse), occasionally the beard of a goat, with one long sharp-pointed horn growing from the middle of its forehead. The unicorn is said to have been identified in India, later noted in early Greek writings and catalogued in the medieval bestiaries. Adopted by the Scots as part of their royal arms, it was later contributed by them to the royal arms of Great Britain, where it shared honors with the lion. Unicorn horns were greatly prized especially by those who had need to guard against hasty ambitions of friends and relatives who might be tempted to use poison as a lever to power, or glory, or riches, or all three. Being extremely sensitive to poison, the unicorn's horn made an ideal drinking vessel. Powdered horn was considered a positive antidote for poison. Even the decorative use of a unicorn on an ordinary drinking cup was a guarantee of protection. Such fanciful beliefs as these persisted through most if not all of the seventeenth century.

Violet

This lovely little purple, blue, yellow or white flower of exquisite fragrance has been extravagantly praised by poets. "The lover's flower," it has been considered emblematic of the sweet virtues of modesty, constancy and devotion. Holme defined a violet as "a small viola" in 1688.

Wallflower

"The wall-flower hath been called by the Herbalists Dames-Violets, Damasen or Matron-Violets or Queens Gillyflowers." (Bayly, 1650) A species of related wild flowers is to be found on old stone walls, in quarries and other places where rocks abound. The red, yellow, orange or purple flowers grow in clusters.

Wheat

This grain is one of the oldest and most widely distributed of the major cereals. Flour derives its name from "flower of the grain," the heart or best part of it. Originating in southeast Asia, it was brought to the western world via Mexico by the Spanish in the 1500's. Later, English settlers introduced it to Virginia and Massachusetts, with indifferent results. In the Midwest, however, it became an important food crop. Bread-baking by public bakers began about 200 B.C. During the Middle Ages a baker might be nailed to his doorpost by his ear for infractions of the craft's many regulations. A formula for bread-pricing was enacted by the English Parliament in 1266 and remained essentially unchanged for 600 years.

Whipporwill

This bird, a member of the nightjar group of goat-suckers, is called a whipporwill in North America. "The Whip-Poor-Will, or lesser Goat-sucker (is) call'd in Virginia, Whip-Poor-Will, from its Cry." (Edwards, 1747). The odd family name derives from an old belief that the bird's large mouth was admirably suited for nocturnal goat-sucking. Actually, it feeds upon insects scooped up in flight. Its cry is indeed night-jarring.

Woodbine

This is a generic name for various climbing plants—convolvulus, ivy, honeysuckle, etc. It was sometimes applied to the green-flowered Virginia creeper described by John Smith (1624) as "A kinde of wood-bind which runnes upon trees, twining it selfe like a vine; the fruit (when) eaten worketh in the nature of a purge."

Woodpecker

This bird is known in most forested lands throughout the world as a hard worker, well-equipped for his task with powerful neck muscles, short, sturdy legs, long sharp-nailed toes and a hard pointed bill. Two species are known to England: the green woodpecker and the wryneck (from its peculiar neck-twisting habit). North American woodpeckers, including flickers and sapsuckers, are more colorful, the red-headed variety being one of the best known. The largest, most spectacular of all, the ivory-billed woodpecker, which has a large red triangular-shaped crest and black and white body colorings, is thought to have become extinct, perhaps within the past decade. It was native to the southeastern United States. About 1600 a woodpecker was also one who enticed innocents into games of chance.

Wren

This busy little chatterbox, with its cocked tail and doughty air, is one of the smallest of birds, yet occupies a secure niche in folklore and legend. This is the "Jenny Wren" of countless nursery tales, as well as the legendary "King of the Birds." By ancient account the avian kingdom congregated to choose a ruler and decided to give the title to the one who soared to the greatest height. The eagle left the ground, confident of easy victory. Just as he reached the apex of his flight and wheeled to scream his victory to earth a tiny wren which had hitched a ride upon the eagle's back fluttered a few feet higher, whereupon he was crowned king by unanimous acclaim. Wrens wear modest coats of varying shades of brown, highlighted by mottles, speckles or stripes. Almost without exception, they are fine all-year singers.

CHAPTER EIGHT

✿ FOUR ADVANCED DESIGNS

DESIGN III

This versatile design may be used in its entirety for handbags, pictures or cushion-covers. Or you may wish to use an element or two as a spray on a sweater, dress or jacket or as a decorative device for a tablecloth or pair of curtains.

The following paragraphs, keyed into the design by letters and numerals, offer color and stitch suggestions. Note particularly how colors are selected for balance and accent.

DESIGN III

DESIGN III

A. Stitch suggestions may be found in Design Units (Acorns; Small Leaves, pages 160-162; 139-145). Acorn cups in #4 golden brown, kernels in #1, #2 and #3 gold. Olive greens suggested for leaves. Medium values of brown may be introduced into the leaves by the use of small filling stitches.

B. These two flowers are done in long and short. Blue would be an attractive color choice, arranged in value sequences as shown. For the two leaves, follow any of the stitch suggestions in Design Units, Small Leaves (pages 139-145), using a different green from that used in the acorn leaves in A.

C. The three leaves at the base of the pomegranate bear the designations 1 and 2. For these leaves, repeat the olive greens used in A. Leaf 1 is couched in #2 and #3 olive green, tied with #4 rose. The leaves numbered 2 are done with solid chain, knot or outline stitch, using five color values as indicated. Work the body of the pomegranate in long and short, using value sequences in rose as shown. The flower petals at the top are worked in buttonhole or satin stitch, using several values of any of the light greens or of rose. Scatter small seeds in the petals, using value #1 of a contrasting color. For flower center, French knots, #4 gold.

D. Do the two small berries in satin stitch, using two medium values of blue, the tendril in knot stitch, #1 green.

E. This unit will "pull" the design together by combining greens, browns and golds, with rose values as accent notes.

The five petals bear designations keyed to the following notes:

Petals 1: Twisted chain, worked closely, beginning with one row of #1 brown (along the dotted line), followed by green from #1 to #5 in value sequences shown.

Petal 2: Run outline stitches around this petal in #3 green, then fill with #3 brown, herringbone, tied with #4 rose.

Petals 3: Outline each petal with small open chain stitches in #3 green, then satin-stitch the center rows in #3 gold.

F. There are two F units in this design: one on the right side, one on the left. These two units may be used to balance the golds and browns in Unit A. Do the two flower buds in long and short, with gold values, the pair of base leaves in Cretan stitch in #2 brown. The two large leaves on the stem (of the right-hand unit only) should balance the greens and browns in Unit A. Stitch suggestions may be found in Design Units, under Small Leaves (pages 139-145).

G. First, use small running stitches to outline the crescent-shaped borders around the five petals, then fill the borders with buttonhole stitches in values of rose, as indicated. Do the center leaf in long and short, starting at the tip with #1 rose and working toward the base, using four values of green, as shown. Use stitches of your selection in the other two leaves at base of flower, working them in #3 green. The leaf topping the petal cluster should be done in a green to balance Unit C. Stitch suggestions may be found in Design Units, under Small Leaves (pages 139-145).

H. The six petals of the carnation are done in long and short. Work the top four first, starting at the tips and working toward the base, using #5, #4, #3 and #2 blue and #1 brown in sequence. The lower petals are worked in blue, in the four value sequences shown. The base is laid work in #3 green, with couching in #3 and #4 blue, tied with #3 green.

I. There are two I units in this design: one on the right side, one on the left. Use French knots in values of blue for each berry, as shown.

J. Work the scalloped border in satin stitch, #2 brown, the rest of the leaf in long and short, olive green, using the value sequences shown.

K. Follow suggestions given for a similar open-faced flower in Design Unit 103, using gold values as indicated on each petal.

L. Work the four petals in closed herringbone in a color of your choice, then edge the four petals in outline stitch, using the next lightest value of the same color, and the base of the flower in satin stitch, #3 green.

M. Top leaf of two attached to stem base in #3 olive green herringbone, tied with #4 gold, with outline stitch around leaf in #4 olive green. Bottom leaf in solid knot stitch, using values of green as indicated.

Work all stems in outline stitches placed side by side. Use combinations of lighter values near the top of the design, with the darker ones toward the bottom. A typical combination for the upper stems would be: #1 golden brown for the inside curved edge, #3 green in the center, finishing with #2 green on the opposite edge.

DESIGN IV

The two patterns shown on the pages immediately following are the two halves of a panel design. Trace both patterns, including the short dotted lines on the right and left sides of both patterns, then place the top half over the bottom half so the dotted lines match exactly. You will then have a complete panel about 16 inches long.

Two or three duplications of this panel, laid end to end, will provide attractive designs for panels or bell pulls 32 or 48 inches long.

The two designs may also be used separately. In this case, you would eliminate the partial stem (at the X mark) in the upper portion of the bottom half of the panel. In tracing these designs onto your background material please follow instructions on page 53. The following paragraphs, keyed into the designs by letters, offer suggestions as to stitches and choice of colors.

DESIGN IV, BOTTOM HALF

206

DESIGN IV, TOP HALF

207

DESIGN IV

Bottom Half

A. Outline this leaf, using twisted chain in #3 green. Fill in with any stitch you wish, using #4 rose for the left half, #5 rose for the right half, with outline stitch in dark green for the vein.

B. The top of this flower done in battlemented couching is most effective. Use four gold values, tied in green. Outline the battlemented area, including the curled tendril, with two rows of knot stitches in #2 and #3 green. The three large leaves under the battlemented area are done in long and short, using value sequences of green as shown. The two small leaves at the base are done in solid Rumanian stitch, #4 green.

C. This is a truly fascinating unit to do. First, run three rows of closely worked outline stitches all around it in three values of blue: #3 outside, #2 in the middle, #1 inside. Use satin stitch in rose for small open-faced flowers, satin stitch in blue for buds and satin stitch in gold for berries. Treat the tiny leaves simply, using satin, buttonhole or Cretan stitch.

D. This covers two separate leaves. Refer to Design Units, under Medium Leaves (pages 146-153), for stitch suggestions. To balance the design properly these leaves should be green, with gold accents in the right leaf, rose accents in the left leaf.

E. Do the mounds in solid long and short, beginning at the top with #4 gold and working through values #4 and #3 of green, as indicated.

F. Outline stitch in values #2, #3 and #4 or #3, #4 and #5 of green, as shown. For small stems, do not use value gradations: just #3 green. If this bottom half of the design is to be used alone, eliminate the stem in the top portion of the design (at the X mark).

L. Tendrils in knot stitch, #2 green.

Top Half

F. Same directions as for F of bottom half.

G. The two bottom leaves are identical in treatment, each having three stitch patterns: solid chain in five values of green, as shown, attached buttonhole stitches in #1, #2 and #3 green value bands as indicated and a center section with attached fly stitches in #4 rose, whipped in #3 green. The large upper leaf is first outlined with two rows of knot stitches in #2 and #3 green. The curled portion of the leaf is done in long and short, using #3, #2 and #1 green and #1 rose in sequence. The remaining portion of the leaf is filled with wheat ears in #3 green. Take a tiny back stitch in #4 rose at the base of each wheat ear. The two small leaves remaining are done in long and short, with rose and green values as shown.

H. Edged in closely worked open chains, #3 green, filled with blue seeds in values #3 and #4.

I. Two berries in closely worked French knots, with #2 blue in one, #3 in the other.

J. Long and short in #1 blue, #2, #3 and #4 green, as shown.

K. See Design Unit 101 for suggestions.

L. Tendrils in knot stitch, #2 green.

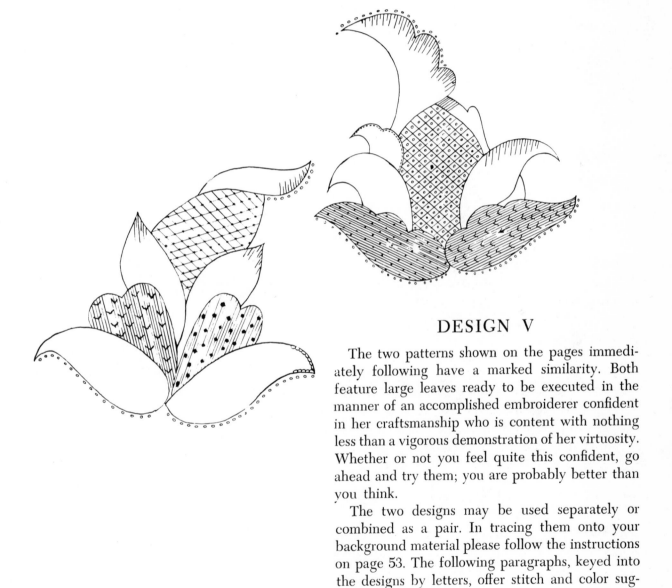

DESIGN V

The two patterns shown on the pages immediately following have a marked similarity. Both feature large leaves ready to be executed in the manner of an accomplished embroiderer confident in her craftsmanship who is content with nothing less than a vigorous demonstration of her virtuosity. Whether or not you feel quite this confident, go ahead and try them; you are probably better than you think.

The two designs may be used separately or combined as a pair. In tracing them onto your background material please follow the instructions on page 53. The following paragraphs, keyed into the designs by letters, offer stitch and color suggestions.

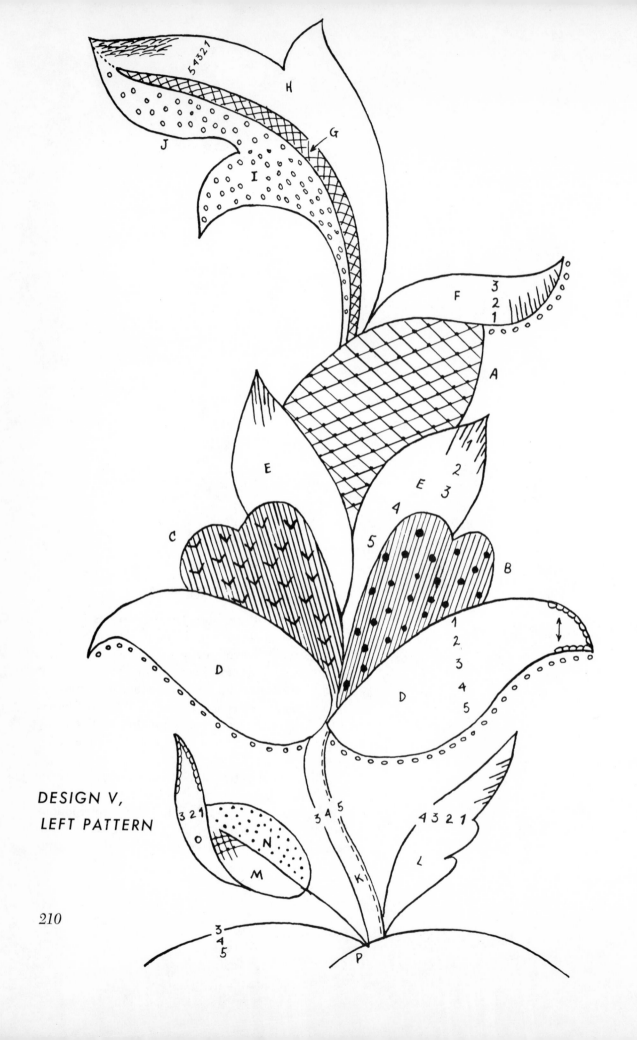

DESIGN V,
LEFT PATTERN

210

DESIGN V,
RIGHT PATTERN

211

DESIGN V

Left Pattern

A. Couch in #2 and #3 green, tie with #3 gold. Outline the couching with one row of twisted chain in #4 green.

B. Laid work in #4 rose, with tie-down stitches in #2 bright yellow green. Run one row of outline stitches around this petal in #5 rose.

C. Laid work in #5 rose, tied down with fly stitches in #2 bright yellow green. Run one row of outline stitches around this petal in #4 rose.

D. Solid chain stitch in values from #1 to #5 of green, as shown. Border the underside of both leaves in French knots in #4 gold.

E. Long and short. Tip in #1 rose, then work from values #1 to #5 of blue green.

F. Long and short. Tip lower edge in #1 gold, then work up through values #1, #2 and #3 of green. Border underside of leaf in French knots, #4 rose.

G. Closed herringbone in #5 rose.

H. Solid outline stitch in values from #1 to #5 of blue green, as shown.

I. French knots in #3 green.

J. Two rows of twisted chain stitch in #4 and #5 green.

K. Work stem in solid outline stitch, using values #3, #4 and #5 of green.

L. Long and short. Tip scalloped edge in #1 rose, then work from value #1 to #4 of green, as shown in diagram.

M. Small couching or herringbone in #3 green, tied with #4 gold. Run outline stitch around the edge in #4 blue green.

N. One row of knot stitch in #3 blue green around the edge. Fill with small seeds in #3 gold.

O. Solid twisted chain stitch in values #3, #2 and #1 of blue green.

P. Top the mound with three rows of knot stitches, using #3, #4 and #5 blue green in one and #3, #4 and #5 green in the other. Fill with small scattered seeds in #3 green.

Right Pattern

A. Couch in #2 and #3 green, tie with #4 rose. Center French knots in each square in #3 gold.

B. Laid work in #4 green, tied with fly stitches in #2 green. Border the underside of the leaf in French knots in #4 gold.

C. Repeat B, tie with #2 green seeds. Border the underside of leaf with French knots in #4 gold.

D. Satin or buttonhole stitch in #3 blue green.

E. Long and short. Tip in #1 gold, then work from value #1 to #5 in rose, as shown.

F. Solid knot stitch from value #1 to #5 blue green.

G. Long and short. Tip in #1 gold, then work from value #1 to #5 of green. Do French knots in #4 rose.

H. Use chain stitch from value #1 to #5 of green.

I. Attached wheat ear in #5 rose.

For the rest of the pattern (J, K, L, M, N, O, P) follow the suggestions given in the paragraphs for J, K, L, M, N, O and P accompanying Left Pattern.

DESIGN VI

This is a part of the border design on a Central European christening set dating from about the mid-seventeenth century, as fresh and attractive today as it was three centuries ago. It is typical of the crewel embroidery designs of the time, but the set itself was not embroidered originally in wool yarn. The early piece has a background of rich dark green satin, with the design worked in soft rose, blue, gold and several shades of green. Gold threads were lavishly interwoven.

The same colors used in the original piece; with the exception of the gold threads, can be effectively combined today on a natural-colored background. Carnations adapt beautifully to shades of rose, the pomegranate to gold, while the small three-petaled open-faced flowers are charming in shades of blue. The large open-faced flowers should balance the colors used in the other units.

The full-size reproduction shown here is too long to be accommodated on one page, hence it is shown in two halves. The left half is the top and fits neatly onto the right half as the bottom, where the small arrows point.

DESIGN V I,
TOP HALF

214

DESIGN VI,
BOTTOM HALF

215

CHAPTER NINE

FINISHING AND BLOCKING

No matter how carefully you have handled your embroidery work it is quite likely to be somewhat soiled by the time it is completed. It is not mandatory that it be washed, but this is usually a good idea.

Do *not* put in a washing machine. Dip it in a basin of lukewarm, mild soapsuds, kneading the piece until you feel that most of the dirt has been removed. (How surprised you will probably be at the color of the water!) Gently squeeze the suds from this first soaping. If you feel that another sudsing would be helpful, do it again, using fresh lukewarm water and suds. Finally, rinse the piece thoroughly in clear lukewarm water. *Caution:* Do not at any time allow the piece to soak in the water.

When thoroughly rinsed, roll it into turkish toweling just as you would a fine sweater. When the toweling has absorbed the excess water, remove the embroidery and carefully smooth out the wrinkles and puckers in the wet piece. Then set it aside to dry. During the drying period you should occasionally pull and straighten it to its proper shape.

When the piece is absolutely dry it is ready for blocking. This is done by stretching it over a board. The board may be natural wood, plywood or some form of composition board, provided it is large enough to provide a firm foundation for the entire piece and sturdy enough to hold tacks under considerable tension. Be sure the tacks are the nonrust type—copper, brass or chrome. Slender-shanked tacks are the easiest to work with.

First, cover the board with a layer or two of waxed paper or aluminum foil. This barrier between embroidery and board guards against possible stains from the wood and reduces water absorption by the board during the final wetting operation.

Now, stretch your piece of twill over the board, securing it firmly by tacks spaced about 1″ apart. Tack along the outside margins of your piece; do not come in next to the embroidery. The whole piece must be stretched.

Start with a tack in the upper lefthand corner (point A). From this point secure the entire top edge (A to B), stretching it tight as you go along. Then, repeat the process along the lefthand edge (A to C), then along the bottom (C to D) and finally along the righthand edge (B to D). All the while you will be pulling the material as tight as you can but taking care not to distort the design. If you have a helpful neighbor or friend, this is the time to call upon her to lend a hand; two can do it easier than one. When you have completed this operation the piece will lie straight and true in every direction without a wrinkle or pucker in sight. By this time you may be slightly weary, so rest a moment while you take time out to admire your creation—finished at last!

With the piece stretched taut, tacked down tight, with the design lined up properly and no puckers or wrinkles in evidence, it is ready for the wetting down. With medium-warm water and a sponge carefully saturate every inch of the material. Do not make the mistake of just wetting the embroidery, for this will cause watermarks to show and the finished piece, when dry, may not be wrinkle-free. Take special care with the embroidery, for wool is difficult to wet thoroughly.

When the whole piece is thoroughly soaked, mop up the excess water with paper towels or a clean absorbent cloth, pressing the toweling down to pick up as much water as possible. Let dry for about 24 hours, then remove the tacks and, believe

it or not, every colorful stitch will stand out in bold relief.

Your piece is now ready for its final destiny: chair seat, framed picture, eyeglass case, portfolio cover, tea cozy or whatever. Whenever a colorful edging would provide a nice finishing touch, as in a portfolio cover or eyeglass case—a border of twisted cord or knot stitches might be added in a matching color.

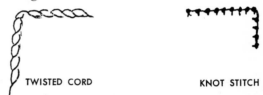

TWISTED CORD   KNOT STITCH

Twisted cord may have from four to eight strands of yarn and is sewed around the edges. Knot stitches are worked into the piece, using two strands in the needle. Color harmony is, of course, essential.

If the piece of embroidery is to be framed as a picture, a frame should be used which is definitely subordinated to the embroidery in size, in design and in color. The frame should complement, not dominate the scene. And a frame without glass is so much more effective.

Note: You may want to identify and date your completed piece of embroidery in some way, perhaps with your name or initials as well as the year in tiny stitches, in an inconspicuous place where it will not detract from the over-all effect.

Tacking and stretching. Use a flat board, with waxed paper or aluminum foil between the embroidery and the board.

When tacked securely and stretched evenly, the piece is ready for wetting. It should be saturated thoroughly.

EPILOGUE

Thus hoping that these workes
    may have this guide,
To serve for ornament, and not for pride:
To Cherish vertue, banish idlenesse,
For these ends, may this booke
    have good success.

The Needle's Excellency
by John Taylor (1580-1653)

SOURCES AND SUPPLEMENTARY TITLES

Adventure in Stitches, Mariska Karasz, Funk & Wagnall, 1959.

Adventures in Embroidery, Ernest Thesiger, The Studio, London, New York, 1942.

American Needlework: The History of Decorative Stitchery from the Late 16th to the 20th Century, Georgiana Brown Harbeson, Bonanza Books, New York, 1961.

Anatomie of Melancholy, Robert Burton, Chatto & Windus, London, 1891.

Bayeux Tapestry, The, Sir Frank Stenton and Francis Wormald.

"Bed Hangings," Abbott Lowell Cummings, for The Society for the Preservation of New England Antiquities, 1961.

Bestiary: A Book of Beasts, Terence H. White, editor, Putnam, New York, 1954. Capricorn Books, 1960.

Birds of the World, Oliver L. Austin, Jr., illustrated by Arthur Singer, Golden Press, New York, 1961.

British Birds, Thomas Bewick, Vol. I, *Land Birds* (1797), Vol. II, *Sea Birds* (1805). Memorial Edition, Quaritch, London, 1885.

Catalogue of English Domestic Embroidery, John L. Nevinson, Victoria & Albert Museum, London, 1938, 1950.

"Commercial Embroideries of Gujarat in the 17th Century," *Journal of the Indian Society of Oriental Art*, Vol. 17, 1949.

"Crewel Craft in English Embroidery," pamphlet issued by Arthur H. Lee & Sons Ltd., New York, Birkenhead, England.

Customs and Fashions in Old New England, Alice Morse Earle, Charles Scribner's Sons, New York, 1893.

Dean, Beryl, *Church Needlework*.

Decorative Motives of Oriental Art, Katherine M. Ball, Joan Lane, Dodd, Mead and Co., London, 1927.

Designing a Book Jacket, Peter Curl, The Studio Ltd., London, 1956.

Development of Embroidery in America, The, Candace Wheeler, Harper & Brothers, New York, 1921.

Dictionary of Embroidery Stitches, Mary Thomas, Hodder & Stoughton Ltd., London, 1934.

Dictionary of Phrase and Fable, E. Cobham Brewster, J. P. Lippincott, Philadelphia.

Early American Textiles, Frances Little, The Century Company, 1931.

Elizabethan Embroideries, Victoria & Albert Museum, London, 1948.

Embroidery and Needlework: A Textbook on Design and Technique, Gladys Windsor Fry, Sir Isaac Pitman & Sons, London, 1935.

Encyclopedia Britannica.

Encyclopedia of Needlework, Therese de Dillmont, editor, Mulhouse (Alsace), E. and P. Verges, 1888-.

English and Other Needlework, Tapestries and Textiles in the Irwin Untermyer Collection, Yvonne Hackenbroch, published for the Metropolitan Museum of Art, Harvard University Press, Cambridge, 1960.

English Costume in the Age of Elizabeth, Iris Brooke, A. and C. Black Ltd., London.

English Country Houses in Colour, A. F. Kersting and Ralph Dutton, Hastings House, New York, 1958.

English Domestic Needlework, Therle Hughes, Macmillan.

English Embroidery, A. F. Kendrick, Newnes, London, 1904.

English Needlework, A. F. Kendrick, A. and C. Black Ltd. London, 1933.

Flower Chronicles, Buckner Hollingsworth, Rutgers University Press, New Brunswick, N. J., 1958.

Flower Embroidery, Kay Kohler, Vista Books, London, 1960.

Flowers in English Embroidery, Victoria & Albert.Museum, London, 1947.

Flowers of the World in Full Color, Robert S. Lemmon and Charles L. Sherman, Doubleday & Company, New York.

Folklore and Symbolism of Flowers, Plants and Trees, The, Ernst and Johanna Lehner, Tudor, New York, 1960.

History of English Embroidery, The, Barbara J. Morris, Victoria & Albert Museum, London.

History of English Furniture, A, Victoria & Albert Museum, London, 1955.

History of English Secular Embroidery, The, M. Jourdain, Kegan Paul, Trench, Trübner and Co. Ltd., London, 1910.

History of Everyday Things in England, A, Marjorie and C. H. B. Quennell, 4 vols., B. T. Batsford Ltd., London, 1945-48.

Homespun and Blue, Martha G. Stearns, Charles Scribners' Sons, New York, 1940.

Illustrated English Social History, G. M. Trevelyan, 4 vols., Longmans, Green, 1951-52.

Indian Embroidery, Victoria & Albert Museum, London.

John Pinder-Wilson's Standard Guide to Embroidery and Other Needlework.

"Indo-European Embroidery," John Irwin, report of lecture of November 26, 1958 in the *Journal of the Embroiderers' Guild*, London.

"Introduction to Study of 18th Century New England Embroidery," Gertrude Townsend, *Bulletin of Museum of Fine Arts*, Boston, April, 1941.

Jacobean Embroidery, Ada Wentworth Fitzwilliam and A. F. Morris Hands, Kegan Paul, Trench, Trübner and Co., Ltd. London, 1928.

"Jacobean Nostalgia," *Embroidery*, summer 1957.

Mary Thomas Embroidery Book, Mary Thomas, Hodder & Stoughton Ltd., London.

"Medieval Embroidery," *Ciba Review*, Ciba Chemical and Dye Company, Basle, Switzerland, December, 1945.

Merry Monarch: The Life and Likeness of Charles II, Hesketh Pearson, Harper & Brothers, New York, 1960.

Modern Embroidery, Mary Hogarth, The Studio, London, 1933.

Modern Needlework, Daily Express, London.

Needle in Hand, Martha G. Stearns, Washburn, New York, 1950.

"New England Crewel Embroideries," Adolph S. Cavallo, *Connecticut Historical Society Bulletin*, April, 1959.

"Notes on Elizabethan Embroidery," Gertrude Townsend, *Bulletin of Museum of Fine Arts*, Boston, April, 1942.

Old English Embroidery, Frances and Hugh Marshall, 1894.

Old English Needlework of the 16th and 17th Centuries, Sidney Hand, Ltd.

"Origins of the Oriental Style in English Decorative Art," John Irwin, *Burlington Magazine*, April, 1955.

Oxford English Dictionary, The.

Pageant of Elizabethan England, The, Elizabeth Burton, Scribner, New York, 1959.

Picture Book of English Embroideries, A: Part I, Elizabethan; Part II, Stuart; Part III, Georgian, 1926, 1928, Victoria & Albert Museum, London.

Romance of Textiles, Ethel Lewis, Macmillan, 1937.

Samplers and Stitches: A Handbook of the Embroiderer's Art, Mrs. Archibald Christie, B. T. Batsford, London, 1920, 7th impression, 1959.

Shakespeare Garden, The, Esther Singleton, The Century Company, New York, 1922.

Shakespeare's England, Clarendon Press, Oxford, 1916.

Symbolism of Animals and Birds in English Church Architecture, Arthur Henry Collins, Sir Isaac Pitman & Sons Ltd., 1913.

Tools and Toys of Stitches, The, Gertrude Whiting, Columbia University Press, 1928.

Tudors, The, Christopher Morris, Macmillan, New York, 1955.

Works of John Taylor, The, edited by Charles Hindley, printed by C. S. Simms, for the Spenser Society, Manchester, 1870.